APR 2 8 2011

S0-AEI-971

East Meadow Public Library
1886 Front Street, East Meadow, NY 11554
(516) 794-2570
www.eastmeadow.info

SURVIVING THE BOND BEAR MARKET

Bondland's Nuclear Winter

MARILYN COHEN AND
CHRIS MALBURG

Publishers of *Marilyn Cohen's Bond Smart Investor* newsletter

WILEY

John Wiley & Sons, Inc.

Copyright © 2011 by Writers Resource Group, Inc. All rights reserved.

Published by John Wiley & Sons, Inc., Hoboken, New Jersey.
Published simultaneously in Canada.

No part of this publication may be reproduced, stored in a retrieval system, or transmitted in any form or by any means, electronic, mechanical, photocopying, recording, scanning, or otherwise, except as permitted under Section 107 or 108 of the 1976 United States Copyright Act, without either the prior written permission of the Publisher, or authorization through payment of the appropriate per-copy fee to the Copyright Clearance Center, Inc., 222 Rosewood Drive, Danvers, MA 01923, (978) 750-8400, fax (978) 646-8600, or on the Web at www .copyright.com. Requests to the Publisher for permission should be addressed to the Permissions Department, John Wiley & Sons, Inc., 111 River Street, Hoboken, NJ 07030, (201) 748-6011, fax (201) 748-6008, or online at http://www.wiley.com/go/permissions.

Limit of Liability/Disclaimer of Warranty: While the publisher and author have used their best efforts in preparing this book, they make no representations or warranties with respect to the accuracy or completeness of the contents of this book and specifically disclaim any implied warranties of merchantability or fitness for a particular purpose. No warranty may be created or extended by sales representatives or written sales materials. The advice and strategies contained herein may not be suitable for your situation. You should consult with a professional where appropriate. Neither the publisher nor author shall be liable for any loss of profit or any other commercial damages, including but not limited to special, incidental, consequential, or other damages.

For general information on our other products and services or for technical support, please contact our Customer Care Department within the United States at (800) 762-2974, outside the United States at (317) 572-3993 or fax (317) 572-4002.

Wiley also publishes its books in a variety of electronic formats. Some content that appears in print may not be available in electronic books. For more information about Wiley products, visit our web site at www.wiley.com.

Library of Congress Cataloging-in-Publication Data:

Cohen, Marilyn.
  Surviving the bond bear market : bondland's nuclear winter / Marilyn Cohen and
Chris Malburg.
     p. cm.
  Includes index.
  ISBN 978-0-470-93752-5 (cloth); ISBN 978-1-118-06400-9 (ebk); ISBN 978-1-118-06401-6 (ebk); 978-1-118-06402-3 (ebk)
     1. Bonds. 2. Portfolio management.   I. Malburg, Christopher R.   II. Title.
HG4651.C6925 2011
332.63'23—dc22

                                                                        2010051397

Printed in the United States of America

10 9 8 7 6 5 4 3 2 1

To Lyssa,

For 26 years, you have been my secretary, assistant, head of operations, friend, and confidante. No matter what I've asked of you or required, you've always done your best. You are my right hand, my left hand. Your work ethic, loyalty, and humanity make you one-in-a-million. My success is partly due to you. For all of the above, I am eternally grateful.

Your boss, your admirer, and your appreciative friend,

Marilyn

Contents

Foreword

The Baby Boom started in 1946, and continued through 1964. Boomers saw their first instance of a financial bubble in the 1970s when gold was finally released from its permanent fix to the dollar and was allowed to float. It went from $42 to $900 in a decade; then it collapsed throughout the 1980s.

After the gold bubble of the 1970s, Boomers and others swore they would never get caught up in another bubble of something so frivolous as gold. "No, no," they said, "from now on we only invest in things that actually have earnings, like technology stocks."

After the Internet bubble hit its peak in 2000, Boomers swore they would never invest in something so ephemeral as Internet stocks. They swore, "From now on, we'll stick with safe investments. Hard assets. Real estate. That's the ticket."

And then, after the 2007 peak of the real estate bubble led to a collapse of the stock market and a deep economic slowdown, Boomers again made their resolutions to never again get caught up in speculative investments. "No, no, from now on," the Boomers promised whoever would listen, "we're really sticking to safe instruments—bonds. After all, people are supposed to invest more in bonds when they get older, aren't they? We're not getting any younger."

Surviving the Bond Bear Market addresses the massive flows into bonds and bond funds of all types. This book clearly and easily takes you through the necessary steps to rebalance your portfolio as the bond market generational cycle changes.

The problem is that the Baby Boomers are such a large group that whenever they all try crowding into the same asset class, the investing public cannot counterbalance their enormous combined weight. Some interesting disruptions occur in the financial markets when the Boomers all decide that bonds are the place to be.

This new investing fashion that has Boomers piling into bonds arrives just as interest rates are nearing the bottom of the 60-year cycle in interest rates. One important point to remember is that bond yields move inversely compared to bond prices. So seeing bond yields fall like this is another way of saying that bond prices are rising.

The following chart looks at the history of high-grade corporate bond yields, dating back as far as 1768 (see Figure F.1).

Notice the significant bottoms for interest rates seen near the decadal marks of 1770, 1830, 1890, and 1950. Each of these bottoms arrives approximately 60 years after the prior one. The next major bottom for interest rates is ideally due in 2010, plus or minus. This cycle expectation just happens to coincide with the arrival of Baby Boomers at an age when they figure they ought to load up on bonds, just to be safe. So once again, Boomers are all piling into another financial asset type at precisely the wrong time—as they did with gold, Internet stocks, and real estate.

There are still ways that Baby Boomers and others can earn income on their money and preserve their capital, but it is not by owning long-term

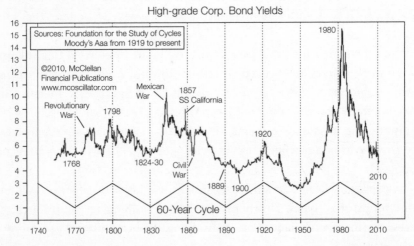

Figure F.1   Sixty-Year Cycle

Source: *The McClellan Market Report* © 2010. All rights reserved. Used with permission.

bonds and bond funds. The question for investors is whether they are going to learn the keys to survival, or get steamrolled by history like everyone else. *Surviving the Bond Bear Market* introduces the concept of bond "duration," and teaches you how you can manage your portfolio's sensitivity as we come out of the bottom for yields in this powerful 60-year cycle. Follow along as Neo Fyte learns the ropes from El Greedo and becomes a sophisticated bond investor in the process.

We have known Marilyn Cohen for many years, and are pleased to introduce to you her latest work. Marilyn started managing bond portfolios back in 1979, just ahead of the bottom for bond prices (and top for yields) in 1980. The past three decades have been a great time to compound the returns on bond portfolios. But Marilyn recognizes that we are at a turning point, and the next three decades will be wholly different. Investors will need to start worrying less about return *on* capital, and worry more about return *of* capital.

Investors who fail to recognize and adjust to the tectonic changes in the bond market are destined to see a long grinding decline in the returns on their investments, and in the value of their money. And there is no time left in this 60-year cycle for Boomers to make up their losses. We highly recommend that you read the book, use the automated e-workbook, and follow Marilyn's advice.

Tom McClellan and Sherman McClellan
The McClellan Market Report
www.mcoscillator.com

Preface

Comparing a bond bear market to a nuclear bomb blast gets everyone's attention. That's our call to action. Bond investors historically had a set-it-and-forget-it approach to their portfolios. At one time that was fine. However, as the 20-year debt binge the United States has been on comes to a crashing halt, the next phase will be *reflation*.

We foresee interest rates spiking, as credit becomes increasingly expensive. Unless the unbridled governmental spending spree ceases, the bond market will come apart. Our idea of the bond market nuclear winter occurs when the U.S. economy heats up again. Interest rates rise, prices rise, employment improves, housing improves—and the bond market dives. Conversely, when the U.S. economy hits a series of increasingly large speed bumps, the bond market takes flight and soars. Simply put, what's good for the general economy is disastrous for the bond market.

The Bond Market Nuclear Winter may take several paths. Higher interest rates could drive bond prices down and portfolio values along with them. Interest rates may remain low or even fall further, forcing investors to reinvest at lower yields. Japan continues to suffer from such fallout. There will be a credit meltdown in the municipal bond space that will create collateral damage in other sectors. Regardless, after reading *Surviving the Bond Bear Market* you'll be prepared. We want you to be the last person standing as the bond market collapses around you.

With this collapse, the set-it-and-forget-it approach to bond portfolio management will be devastating to the unprepared. These individual investors will not survive the ensuing nuclear winter of the bond bear market. Their investment portfolios will crash in value.

The United States has increased its debt burden to historic levels. So many states, cities, and counties suffer from deficit spending. There seems to be no end in sight. The politicians haven't yet shut off the money spigot that ensures their reelection term after term. California with its $25 billion deficit is a bad example of a deplorable scenario.

During 2008 through 2009, the securities markets suffered the worst credit crisis in recent history. Without any break in the bad news came the sovereign debt crisis of 2009 through 2010. The third crisis is coming. It will be that of America's public finance. Along with government spending, it results from overpaid union and public employees who were, and still are, promised unrealistic retirement packages. Too many of their municipal employers have left the pension funds deeply underfunded. Others have built into their funding models ridiculous investment projections of 8 percent and more in a 3 percent world.

As a result, we anticipate a rapidly deteriorating municipal bond market within the next several years. Once this slide begins, we see it gathering momentum until munis crash like an errant meteor into the seabed. The market will likely stay there for some time while the United States figures a way out. The climb back up to where we once were will be a long one—the bond market equivalent of a nuclear winter that may last far longer than anyone expects.

How will individual investors recognize the beginnings of the bond bear market? What should you do to prevent yet another catastrophe in your investment portfolio? How do you retain sufficient investment income to ride out the nuclear winter while still meeting your financial obligations? Finally, how do you recognize the green shoots of the bond market recovery? What must you do to take advantage of the opportunities? *Surviving the Bond Bear Market* answers each of these questions in plain English.

In our earlier book, *Bonds Now!*, we described the new, post-meltdown bond market landscape and how to use the new rules of bond investing to stabilize your bond portfolio. With that knowledge, you've built a stable bond portfolio. However, neither you nor anyone else could have anticipated the confluence of negatives that are now driving the bond market toward the edge of a very sheer cliff. Standing at the edge of that cliff is where *Surviving the Bond Bear Market* jumps off.

We wrote this book for individual investors who are experienced in the bond market. You know what a bond is and how it works and have likely owned corporates, munis, zeros, and bond funds in your investment portfolio. In short, you appreciate the bond market's intricacies and the oncoming dangers. But, you might never have managed a bond portfolio during a bear market in bonds.

Investors have struggled to rebuild their bond portfolios. They have learned how to invest in the new bond landscape. The problem is that very dark cloud looming on the bond horizon. We want you to prepare for it, recognize its arrival, and survive its wrath. That is what *Surviving the Bond Bear Market* will do for you.

Chapter by chapter, the book walks you through the signposts warning of the treacherous road ahead. After studying *Surviving the Bond Bear Market*, you'll be able to see the potential results of the coming nuclear winter before it occurs and with enough time to build a fallout shelter for your bond portfolio. You'll learn how to judge for yourself the severity of the coming crisis and how yield curve inflection points provide very real signals if you know how to read them. The book recognizes there will be some casualties in every bond portfolio before the cataclysm hits bottom. We dedicate an entire chapter to financial triage—surgical removal of your greatest bond risks in the coming environment.

No one can predict the timing of a bond market collapse or foretell which sectors will suffer most. We want to prepare you for the worst even as we hope for the best. We've described the worst—not being able to reinvest at yields that provide a livable income for an investment portfolio whose value lies in ruin. There may be an in between—where the reduction in bond yields simply chokes your finances rather than throwing you out on the streets.

The character of El Greedo, whom we introduced in *Bonds Now!*, continues to receive fan mail. El's sympathizers will be pleased to know he's back in *Surviving the Bond Bear Market* along with a new associate—his brother-in-law, Neo Fyte. Together, they humanize and shoulder the strain from a task that can be daunting.

Surviving the Bond Bear Market describes, informs, and identifies specific actions for bond investors. You will find our Action Steps scattered throughout the book with your hazmat team leader in his insulated suit. Here's how they work:

ACTION STEP

Throughout the book you'll see boxes labeled Action Step. These are specific instructions—summarized in plain English—that tell you just what to do. Action Steps convert the theory discussed in the text to practical use in your bond portfolio.

Skeptics may wonder: What if *Surviving the Bond Bear Market* is wrong? At worst, you've learned how to manage your portfolio with preemptive strategies in the event the worst case occurs.

The accompanying e-workbook, included with this purchase for the first time, allows you to consolidate all of your bond brokerage accounts in a single analytical spreadsheet system. It provides a variety of essential bond information presented in easy-to-understand formats, language, and reports—similar to what professional bond managers use every day.

We know you'll enjoy reading *Surviving the Bond Bear Market* as you follow El Greedo and Neo Fyte through their trials. More importantly, we hope that you will use the ideas and concepts to weather the financial challenges about to confront us all.

Chapter 1
WARNING SIGNS

"What do you mean? Cut back? My wife—your sister—doesn't do cut-back."

El Greedo eyeballed his brother-in-law, Neo Fyte, across the hand-stitched Vachetta leather car seat. He had grudgingly hired him as a salesman at Greedo's Partz before he sold the company. That was five years ago.

"Just what I said. Cut back. Now. Before it is too late. Like before, in two-thousand-eight." *Do I really need to spell it out for this guy?* El Greedo wondered.

"But the portfolio is doing fine. You did that rebalance thing. You diversified into municipal bonds. The family has income."

My God, El Greedo thought. *And my sister married this economic moron?* He squeezed the leather-wrapped steering wheel. He knew he would have to trade his beloved BMW for a used Kia shortly.

"Income, yes," said Greedo. "For now. But the bonds are maturing. Too many of the issuers are in trouble; they're scratching for cash, just like we will be.

1

I need to replace those bonds. But with *what?* What is out there that is safe enough and throws off enough income—"

"So what do we do?" asked Neo. "You run the family's money, Mr. Investment Guru. What are you going to do?"

■ ■ ■

As we write *Surviving the Bond Bear Market,* interest rates are still scraping by like an old car muffler clattering along the roadway. However, a number of economic, political, and international influences are about to exert their force in a catastrophic way. Interest rates will inevitably soar. This will launch a devastating assault on the bond market. Fixed income investors—many of them Baby Boomers and elderly retirees—will lose the nest eggs on which they live. There will be a mass redistribution of the world's economic wealth. Much of it will be repatriated back to lenders like China, Japan, and the United Kingdom.

The pain has already started. America's economy even now is causing untold financial hardship and economic suffering among its population. College graduates can't find jobs. Workers with 10, 20 years of service at their companies are laid off with little prospect of finding another job. Homeowners don't have the money to pay their mortgages. Banks are foreclosing on nonperforming loans in droves. They just hope to get their money back. But the real estate buyers aren't coming. States, counties, cities, and other municipalities have run out of money to pay for basic services like fire and police protection. This is the start of the nuclear winter and the accompanying devastation in the bond market.

Sound like a grim picture? We agree. We're professional bond investors. By our nature we always paint the worst-case scenario. We hope we're wrong. However, the warning signs we see and that we'll show you in this first chapter say otherwise. And what if we're wrong? The worst case is that you'll understand what can happen to your bond portfolio under the direst of circumstances and what you can do about it. After reading this book and following the tips given, you'll have a good idea of how to guarantee a fixed income you can count on to be there when you need it.

A Simple Three-Step Approach

Like El Greedo's struggle earlier, you can protect your bond portfolio from disaster. It's not that difficult. After reading this book, we think you'll agree.

The pundits on the financial television shows make it sound unfathomable. It's really not. That's just how they make their living. Come on; follow us, we'll show you the way.

The best approach to protect your fixed income portfolio from outright disaster in the credit markets includes just three steps:

1. Know the signs that tell you when the market has become unstable and is teetering—that's in this chapter and the next.
2. Develop an action plan to insulate your portfolio as the bond bear market unfolds.
3. Identify the green shoots of recovery and develop an investment plan to take advantage of the inherent opportunities.

Taken by themselves none of the three steps are difficult. However, there is one thing that will separate the haves from the have-nots in the coming bond bear market: **believing the warning signs you see and having the courage to execute your survival plan.** We'll show you how to take the definitive actions necessary to save the value of your bond portfolio.

Now is not the time to be weak-kneed and indecisive. Pull in your belly, stick out your chin. Suck it up. Let's roll.

Warning Sign #1: Interest Rates

The Air Force's 53rd Weather Reconnaissance Squadron, the famed Hurricane Hunters, assesses and analyzes oncoming hurricanes. They fly into the teeth of these mega-storms, often packing winds in excess of 100 miles per hour, to accumulate density, wind speeds, ground speeds, trajectory, and all manner of other data. Then they compute when the storm will make landfall and how severe it will be.

Like a hurricane, the bond market's coming nuclear winter without a doubt will be a financial calamity. Like the 53rd Squadron, we know this one is coming. What no one knows is the precise date it will make landfall or just how long it will last.

Interest Rate Movement

Interest rates are at generational lows. They will rise in the foreseeable future. As rates soar, bond prices will plummet. For bond investors who say they will hold their positions until maturity, the rate hike by itself won't affect them all that much—until it happens.

The scary part of rocketing interest rates is the devastation it brings to *portfolio values*. This is a psychologically damaging event for investors. How would you like to see the value of your bond portfolio drop by half over a short period—say just three months? It could happen.

Investors will begin wondering if it will ever come back. They'll begin to feel poor, at least less wealthy. Investors are also consumers. They will consume less. And they will worry how to recoup their losses. Then the real concern surfaces: As if portfolio erosion wasn't bad enough, what happens if the bonds begin to default? That loss of principal along with the devastated portfolio value will send bond investors into pure, unadulterated panic.

Attempting to save the value of their portfolios, they'll begin selling into a plunging market—ostensibly before it goes any lower. Investors will trade bonds they know, have lived with for some time, and whose coupon payment history hasn't yet been compromised. Investors will console themselves that at least they stopped the hemorrhaging. No, they didn't.

What If Interest Rates Don't Soar?   There's a second possibility for the nuclear winter: Interest rates remain low for some time like they have in Japan for the past 20 years. This presents an altogether different problem for bond investors. Here's how:

Let's say that you bought bonds during the days of high interest rates. Your bonds pay higher interest. If you're like most people, you've become used to that income stream. You've probably adapted your lifestyle to spend up to the level of that income stream. Like El Greedo and his seemingly economically naive brother-in-law, Neo Fyte, Baby Boomers don't know how to cut back. As interest rates remain low, bonds are called or they mature out of their portfolios. Either way, they must be replaced. As Greedo pleaded, "But with *what?*"

The bonds you replace will generate much lower income. That income won't support your current lifestyle and financial commitments. Something will have to change. Since investors can't force bond income up, it is we who must cut our spending. The good news is we have that ability. America's cash-strapped cities, counties, and states apparently do not.

People invested in bond funds will be in a worse position. The public piling into bond funds for a few extra morsels of yield will quickly see their dividend distributions ratcheted down.

ACTION STEP: KEEP YOUR EYE ON INTEREST RATES

Everyone seems to have their own pet ways of predicting interest rate movements. We want your assessment to be more quantitatively rigorous than just watching the evening news for their take. They don't know. Table 1.1 shows the eight primary drivers of changes in interest rates, what they mean, and where to find them.

Table 1.1 Interest Rate Warning Signs and Where to Find Them

Interest Rates Drivers	What They Mean	Source of Information
Unemployment rates	If unemployment falls, then consumer spending increases, driving up demand for borrowing as well as interest rates. If unemployment continues to stay the same, then it indicates interest rates just may continue at their lows.	The official government unemployment rate comes out at 8:30 A.M. EST on the first Friday of every month. Find it in the business section of any newspaper or the *Wall Street Journal*.
Housing starts and sales	Watch for the housing starts and sales to stop falling and become firm or even rise. When this happens, interest rates will start upward. If it remains the same, then look for interest rates to languish at the bottom.	The U.S. Census Bureau releases housing information every month around the 17th at 8:30 A.M. EST. Find it on the web site, http://www.census.gov/const/www/newressalesindex.html.
Consumer Confidence Index	Watch for the Consumer Confidence Index to start rising. When this happens, interest rates will start upward.	The Conference Board releases consumer confidence information every month on the last Tuesday. Find it on their web site, www.conference-board.org/economics/consumerconfidence.cfm.

(Continued)

Table 1.1 (*Continued*)

Interest Rates Drivers	What They Mean	Source of Information
Treasury yields	Movement in Treasury yields usually precedes a move by the Federal Reserve to increase interest rates.	Find Treasury yields at www.bloomberg.com.
Federal debt	Increased federal debt adds to the deficit in both principal and interest. The federal government may allow the value of the U.S. dollar to fall to repay the debt in cheaper dollars. This makes foreign governments less willing to buy Treasury bonds, thus raising interest rates.	Numerous places have the federal debt. An easy web site is Treasury Direct at http://www.treasurydirect.gov/NP/BPDLogin?application=np.
Bond fund flows	Indicates investor sentiment as well as their hunger for yield. As interest rates rise (or at the expectation of a rise), the value of bond funds falls. Investors scramble for the exits.	Every week, the *Wall Street Journal* (and WSJ Online) prints bond fund flow information.
Treasury International Capital (TIC figure)	The TIC identifies the amount and holder of U.S. debt owned by foreigners.	U.S. Department of Treasury, Treasury International Capital web site at http://www.ustreas.gov/tic. Click on quarterly analysis and results.
Corporate bond spreads	As corporate bond spreads increase, interest rates are likely to rise and vice versa.	Spreads appear in *Barron's* weekly.

Source: Envision Capital Management, Inc. Used with permission.

Warning Sign #2: Credit Problems

Credit problems in 2010 were occurring in the municipal bond market. The problem was, you couldn't tell by the low yields. One cause of the bond bear market will be that institutions as well as individual investors who would normally buy and hold bonds will withdraw their normal goodwill. It begins simply with investors demanding compensation for the risk they take in the form of higher interest rates. El Greedo would say, "If you don't balance your budget, I won't lend you my money—the time for smoke and mirrors is over." This attitude among bond investors will make floating a new bond issue far more costly for municipalities.

Investors in municipal bonds will become very choosy. They will compete for those issues having the best credit ratings and shun those that don't. Such a credit crunch will have the effect of locking out many municipal issuers that desperately need cash. Without that money, they will literally go broke.

This started a number of negative effects that began in 2010:

- **Cutting the expense of public employees.** Massive layoffs, work weeks cut, employees going on mandatory furlough, public employee salaries cut.

- **Failing to contribute to employee pension funds.** This will continue to exacerbate the already-egregious national disgrace of unfunded public employee pensions.

- **Noticeable reduction in municipal services** like police and fire protection, and curtailed operation of city halls and libraries.

- **Cities will defer needed maintenance** on their roads, buildings, and other infrastructure because they no longer have the money to pay for it. Our cities, once a source of national pride, will become shabby and neglected.

Those municipalities not locked out of the credit markets completely will have to pay higher interest rates to the point where it becomes cost prohibitive. Some will incur such high interest costs that they will have to raise taxes and issue yet more bonds just to keep up with the interest of prior bond issues.

Warning Sign #3: Inflation/Deflation

America's national debt stood at over $13 trillion at the time of this writing. It was growing at the rate of $2 million per minute, 24/7. Much of this has to do with the longest wars in U.S. history. According to the respected National Priorities Project, the Iraqi war has cost $783 billion since inception. The Afghanistan war has cost $284 billion since inception. As of mid-2010, that's $1 trillion and change when combined.

Another trillion dollars or so of the national debt resulted from the bank bailouts of 2008/2009 and the stimulus package. A lot of money went to create make-work jobs and compensation for the 9.5 percent of all Americans who were unemployed. We'll never recoup any sort of return on that investment.

Paying all this money requires the U.S. Treasury to issue massive amounts of debt—to *print money* as some call it. Historically, countries that issue such large amounts of debt inevitably suffer from extended periods of hyperinflation. The inflation rate we anticipate that the United States will experience over the next decade will most certainly extend the bond market's nuclear winter.

Debt

U.S. households have never been deeper in debt. According to *Barron's*, reducing U.S. household debt to a livable 65 percent of income would require Americans to repay the $6.3 trillion they have borrowed. That would require a massive spending reduction. The fact that about 40 percent of our households live hand-to-mouth, spending every last dime they make just to keep their heads above water, guarantees little meaningful debt reduction in the foreseeable future.

When interest rates rise, those same households with adjustable rate mortgages and that live on credit card debt will suffer greatly. An even larger part of their disposable income will go toward interest payments. This will certainly not improve U.S. economic growth.

Expand the dilemma faced by America's households to her states, counties, cities, and other municipalities. Like Greece, our governmental bodies have spent just as irresponsibly. Former California Governor Schwarzenegger asked the federal government for aid twice, once in 2008 and again in 2009. Governor Schwarzenegger desperately needed these funds to pay for the federally mandated education, incarceration, police, fire, and medical care required by illegal aliens flooding California from across the Mexican border. His pleas fell on deaf ears.

Indeed, the debt in some of America's largest cities and states is so high that it will reach a flashpoint. As soon as one of the big municipal bond issuers like California, Los Angeles, New York, New Jersey, or Illinois technically defaults on its bond payments a tsunami will roll through the bond market. Should a big city like Los Angeles declare bankruptcy (as suggested by former LA mayor, Richard Riordan), the other mayors in similar financial straits may be tempted to follow suit.

For Los Angeles, the bankruptcy strategy may make sense. During 2010, LA had unfunded pension liabilities of $2.3 billion and a budget deficit equivalent to 10 percent of the entire city budget. In bankruptcy court a judge would likely cancel some of the ongoing obligations that are sucking up so much cash.

If this happens, the floodgates will open once the first major municipal bond issuer files for bankruptcy. Bond investments will be at extreme risk. Interest rates on new issues will spike and prices will plummet. This conceivably will be one of the explosions that starts the bond market nuclear winter.

Warning Sign #4: Confiscatory Tax Rates

Tax rates are rising. They're going to go even higher. Our elected officials have no choice. The money to pay for both the unbridled spending and the debt to fund it must come from somewhere. That somewhere is taxes—personal income taxes, corporate taxes, sales taxes, property taxes, and new taxes we haven't even heard of yet. The value-added tax (VAT) is surely on its way.

Higher tax rates reduce personal consumption and increase the debt required by American households just to maintain their present standard of living. For those on a fixed income, this will jeopardize their lifestyle and living standards.

Warning Sign #5: Governmental Spending

This is a sore point among an increasingly large group of Americans. Sentiment runs to the more conservative side of the boat—stop governmental spending. However, when the chief of spending sits at the top of the government, most other politicos will follow his lead. Further, that is how officials get themselves reelected—by spending on constituencies they know will vote them back into office.

The political environment has always had a fork in the road. On the one hand, there are painful decisions that are right for the people. On the other hand, there are decisions that just kick problems down the road while keeping incumbents in office. For too many years now, America has elected leaders more inclined to get reelected rather than to make the tough decisions needed to restore fiscal health.

Unfunded pension liabilities are a growing cancer that will surely kill America's fiscal health. A 2010 *Barron's* survey estimated nationwide unfunded pension liabilities at $2 to $3 trillion. New York City's unfunded pension liability was $60 billion from the same survey. Such astronomical figures illustrate the size of the crater the bond market will create when it finally explodes.

This problem occurred partly due to the type of pension plan granted to public employees. Too many public pension plans include a cost-of-living increase and lifetime health care, making the future liability uncertain and difficult to predict. Defined benefit plans, on the other hand, have no such inflation protection—bad for the pensioner, but it makes a more manageable pension liability for the public entity. This difference ensures that the unfunded liability problem will continue to increase as the Obama Administration cranks up its policy of future inflation at any cost to the next generation.

Yes, municipalities are switching to defined benefit plans for their new employees. However, the problem rests not with the newbies, but with the millions of already-retired government pensioners with undefined benefit plans. These people often draw more than their former salaries thanks to accumulated bumps in cost-of-living allowances.

There are almost as many ways to measure governmental spending as there are economists to do it. We measure governmental spending in just two simple ways:

- Outstanding debt
- Budget deficit

We figure if the debt is increasing, then spending is probably increasing, too. It's the same with budget deficits: If deficits are increasing, so is governmental spending. Find out your state's budget deficit and its total debt on your state's web site. Use that increase as a warning sign.

Warning Sign #6: Foreign Influences

The U.S. economy is heavily dependent on the goodwill of foreign governments. Many foreign governments are not friendly to our cause. Our largest creditors are China, Japan, and the United Kingdom. As with most banking relationships, this one follows its own golden rule: He who has the gold makes the rules. In this case, the gold resides with America's creditors, not with us. China, for example, owns about $900 billion of U.S. Treasury bonds (Reuters as of June 23, 2010). This position gives China the ability to demand greater fiscal prudence in the form of lower deficits.

Failure to comply with our banker's demands would mean economic catastrophe. China may reduce its asset allocation of U.S. Treasurys if we don't exercise greater fiscal prudence. The damage of this action would ripple through all major U.S. credit markets. It would create the following chain reaction:

- The U.S. Treasury will have to raise the interest rate offered on Treasury debt to entice buyers. This would further increase the U.S. deficit.

- The U.S. corporate bond market follows the Treasury market. This will drive bond prices down. The value of bond portfolios and bond funds will plummet. This will be a complete disaster for already-nervous bond investors. They will panic and dump their bond investments, causing another precipitous drop in the bond market.

- The market for mortgage-backed securities will plunge in value. This will drive mortgage rates up. Higher mortgage rates make it more expensive to buy real estate or refinance it. This will further reduce the number of qualified first-time homebuyers.

- The commercial credit market will raise the cost of capital to compensate lenders for higher perceived risk. This makes it more expensive for U.S. business to expand. A general business contraction will ensue.

Using the TIC Figure

Around the 15th of every month, the U.S. Treasury issues its Treasury International Capital (TIC) figures. These numbers identify the amount of U.S. debt owned by foreigners. For example, the June 15, 2010 TIC report showed that net foreign purchases of long-term U.S. securities was $83 billion.

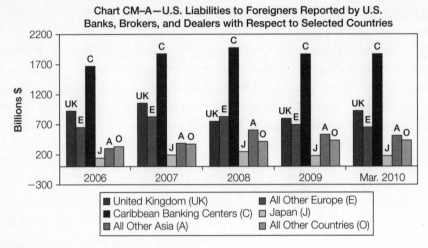

Figure 1.1   U.S. Liabilities to Foreigners
Source: United States Treasury.

The TIC is important because if it keeps on falling, it means foreigners are not buying U.S. Treasurys. If prolonged, this situation could become catastrophic for the bond market.

Almost as important as the total amount of U.S. debt owned by foreigners is *who* owns it. Are they our friends or foes? For example, Figure 1.1 shows the U.S. Treasury debt ownership as of March 2010.

Warning Sign #7: Bond Fund Flows

An excellent warning sign for expectations of interest rate movement is the flow of money into and out of bond funds. When interest rates begin climbing, net asset values will plummet. Bond fund investors will scramble for the exits. Fund values will drop almost as fast as Tiger Woods's reputation.

If you're a bond fund investor, you have a vested interest in watching this flow of funds indicator. When the cash flow into bond funds slows down, everyone pays attention. It means the nervous money is afraid of a drop in the bond fund value due to an expectation of higher interest rates.

When you see a trend develop over a period of two or three months, you need to reduce your exposure to bond funds. Replace these holdings with the actual bonds. We don't want you to be trampled by others rushing for the exits when they realize the bond fund bubble has finally burst.

Warning Sign #8: Bond Spreads

Spreads in corporate and municipal bonds relative to Treasury yields are called the *bond spread* (or simply, *the spread*). The spread measures the difference in yield between two bonds with the same maturities. Corporate bond spreads trade as *a percentage over* the Treasury yield; municipal bond spreads are *a percentage of* the Treasury yield. The bond spread tells the additional yield required to compensate for added risk.

As spreads fluctuate, they say a great deal about the direction of interest rates as well as investor sentiment related to risk. Fluctuations in spreads can create huge problems for companies and municipalities needing to issue bonds. For example, during November, December 2008, and January 2009, there was wild fluctuation in the spreads (perceived risk) of munis to Treasurys.

And for good reason: With the downfall of Lehman Brothers and the looming potential collapse of Citigroup and Bank of America, investors were scared out of their wits that the entire U.S. financial system was coming unglued. The flight to quality was limited to U.S. Treasurys and nothing else. The few investors willing to buy a municipal bond demanded—and received—a huge risk premium. Figures 1.2 through 1.4 are the Bloomberg charts for the three months showing the spreads (look at the right-hand column).

Notice how the spreads rose from November to December—the height of the panic—then began to settle between December and January. That's the information we want to track. Even in January the municipal bond spreads exceeded the yield you could earn on Treasurys. This has happened in the past, but not for such an extended time. It was highly unusual that it lasted so long. However, it will be repeated during the coming bond market troubles.

Find the spreads for corporates and municipal bonds appearing in *Barron's* every week.

```
GRAB                                              Muni  GBY
<TAB> to Select Data for Different Dates
              G.O. MUNICIPAL BONDS
            BLOOMBERG DAILY GENERIC OAS YIELDS      AAA MUNICIPAL
              THURSDAY CLOSE    DATE: 11/13/08         AS % OF
                AAA        AA        A       BAA1    CURRENT US GOVT.'S
             (SECTOR 49) (SECT.104) (SECT.159) (SECT.631)
   1 YR  2009   1.84      1.97      2.39      3.08        165.20
   2 YR  2010   2.36      2.48      2.93      3.53        195.41
   3 YR  2011   2.71      2.85      3.3       3.83        174.78
   4 YR  2012   2.96      3.11      3.53      4.16        168.13
   5 YR  2013   3.16      3.32      3.74      4.45        130.65
   7 YR  2015   3.56      3.72      4.1       4.82        116.32
   9 YR  2017   4.06      4.2       4.6       5.22        109.32
  10 YR  2018   4.32      4.46      4.86      5.54        113.21
  12 YR  2020   4.6       4.77      5.15      6.33        111.45
  14 YR  2022   4.77      4.94      5.31      6.94        107.46
  15 YR  2023   4.86      5.05      5.41      7.14        105.78
  17 YR  2025   5.01      5.17      5.57      7.32        108.92
  19 YR  2027   5.13      5.31      5.7       7.35        111.41
  20 YR  2028   5.14      5.31      5.71      7.35        111.56

  25 YR  2033   5.16      5.35      5.88      7.36        111.80

  30 YR  2038   5.18      5.36      5.89      7.36        118.86
Australia 61 2 9777 8600 Brazil 5511 3048 4500 Europe 44 20 7330 7500 Germany 49 69 9204 1210 Hong Kong 852 2977 6000
Japan 81 3 3201 8900        Singapore 65 6212 1000     U.S. 1 212 318 2000      Copyright 2010 Bloomberg Finance L.P.
                                                                    SN 776233 G407-87-1 14-Jul-10 14:41:48
```

Figure 1.2   Muni Spread (November 2008)

Source: Bloomberg Finance LP. © 2009 Bloomberg Finance LP. All rights reserved. Used with permission.

```
GRAB                                              Muni  GBY
<TAB> to Select Data for Different Dates
              G.O. MUNICIPAL BONDS
            BLOOMBERG DAILY GENERIC OAS YIELDS      AAA MUNICIPAL
              MONDAY CLOSE      DATE: 12/15/08         AS % OF
                AAA        AA        A       BAA1    CURRENT US GOVT.'S
             (SECTOR 49) (SECT.104) (SECT.159) (SECT.631)
   1 YR  2009   1.29      1.42      1.84      2.73        261.19
   2 YR  2010   2.08      2.2       2.65      3.34        285.64
   3 YR  2011   2 ½       2.68      3.13      3.85        246.96
   4 YR  2012   2.86      3.01      3.43      4.2         330.90
   5 YR  2013   3.08      3.24      3.66      4.43        208.90
   7 YR  2015   3.56      3.72      4.1       4.79        209.24
   9 YR  2017   4.15      4.29      4.69      5.37        167.08
  10 YR  2018   4.44      4.58      4.98      5.79        176.46
  12 YR  2020   4.91      5.08      5.46      6.81        171.88
  14 YR  2022   5.13      5 ¼      5.62      7.67        160.46
  15 YR  2023   5.23      5.42      5.78      7.87        155.32
  17 YR  2025   5.45      5.67      6.01      8.05        163.41
  19 YR  2027   5.59      5.77      6.16      8.07        169.23
  20 YR  2028   5.65      5.82      6.22      8.07        171.88

  25 YR  2033   5 ¾      5.94      6.47      8.08        179.13

  30 YR  2038   5.77      5.95      6.48      8.08        195.45
Australia 61 2 9777 8600 Brazil 5511 3048 4500 Europe 44 20 7330 7500 Germany 49 69 9204 1210 Hong Kong 852 2977 6000
Japan 81 3 3201 8900        Singapore 65 6212 1000     U.S. 1 212 318 2000      Copyright 2010 Bloomberg Finance L.P.
                                                                    SN 776233 G407-87-0 14-Jul-10 14:42:33
```

Figure 1.3   Muni Spread (December 2008)

Source: Bloomberg Finance LP. © 2009 Bloomberg Finance LP. All rights reserved. Used with permission.

```
GRAB                                                    Muni  GBY
<TAB> to Select Data for Different Dates
          G.O.  MUNICIPAL  BONDS
          BLOOMBERG DAILY GENERIC OAS YIELDS        AAA MUNICIPAL
          THURSDAY CLOSE    DATE:  1/15/09             AS % OF
            AAA        AA        A        BAA1     CURRENT US GOVT.'S
        (SECTOR 49) (SECT.104) (SECT.159) (SECT.631)
 1 YR  2010    0.69       0.89      1.39      2.47        178.53
 2 YR  2011    1.43       1.62      2.09      2.9         195.57
 3 YR  2012    1.73       1.98      2.45      3.34        171.51
 4 YR  2013    1.87       2.16      2.53      3.72        179.22
 5 YR  2014    2.08       2.36      2 ³₄      4.04        152.05
 7 YR  2016    2.54       2.78      3.17      4.65        164.17
 9 YR  2018    3.18       3.36      3.81      5.49        147.64
10 YR  2019    3.54       3.7       4.17      6.01        159.43
12 YR  2021    3.97       4.17      4.61      7.14        153.12
14 YR  2023    4.11       4.45      4.69      7.88        138.62
15 YR  2024    4.21       4.53      4.85      8.08        133.60
17 YR  2026    4.45       4.65      5.1       8.28        140.39
19 YR  2028    4.59       4.84      5 ¹₄      8.28        143.96
20 YR  2029    4.64       4.88      5.3       8.28        145.10

25 YR  2034    4.71       4.97      5.52      8.28        151.85

30 YR  2039    4.73       4.98      5.53      8.28        164.92
Australia 61 2 9777 8600 Brazil 5511 3048 4500 Europe 44 20 7330 7500 Germany 49 69 9204 1210 Hong Kong 852 2977 6000
Japan 81 3 3201 8900    Singapore 65 6212 1000    U.S. 1 212 318 2000    Copyright 2010 Bloomberg Finance L.P.
                                                   SN 776233 G407-87-0 14-Jul-10 14:43:22
```

Figure 1.4   Muni Spread (January 2009)

Source: Bloomberg Finance LP. © 2009 Bloomberg Finance LP. All rights reserved. Used with permission.

Added Symptoms of Nuclear Winter in Bondland

The first symptom we'll see is a series of disturbing credit defaults and restructures. Sovereign debt is a good example. As we write this book the European Union bailed out Greece to keep it from defaulting on its debt. We see Ireland and Spain needing similar treatment. Ireland's implosion was at full tilt during November 2010.

In mid-2010, U.S. cities were collectively running over $140 billion in budget deficits, according to the Center on Budget and Policy Priorities. To close this humongous budget gap, municipalities would cut expenses or increase borrowing if the municipal bond market were more accommodating. The complaint is usually that it is too little, too late. Nevertheless, to identify whether a particular issuer is in trouble, look for them to try a **massive worker layoff**: During 2010, Los Angeles considered laying off all nonessential city workers. It cut workweeks and also considered reducing its workers' salaries.

Watch for the first major city to default on its debt. It doesn't even have to declare bankruptcy—that's less likely, anyway. A default is the indicator we're looking for. It might be San Diego, Los Angeles, Chicago, or New York. Default, and the negotiations with creditors that follow, will be the test case. If other cities see a forgiveness of debt and some give from the public employee unions with their iron grip on their members' pensions, then we'll see more defaults in rapid succession. This will imperil the bond holders.

Muni Bond Selectivity

The Federal Reserve reported in the first quarter of 2010 that financial institutions owned $216.2 billion in municipal debt. By itself, Citigroup held $13.4 billion of this. State Street Bank owned $6.2 billion. These institutional investors were highly selective in their municipal bond purchases. Nevertheless, they will have to sell many issues when credit problems surface. Even if only 25 percent fall below their investment rating standards and they have to sell, that's $54 billion in unwanted municipal bonds flooding the market almost at once.

This will depress municipal bond values. Investors will panic. What began as a controlled selloff of substandard bonds will turn into all-out terror.

Enter the Bond Vigilantes

Economist, media pundit, and financial seer Ed Yardeni coined the term *bond vigilantes* in the 1980s. They are simply institutional investors who own enormous bond positions in concentrated issues. They sell short the bonds of governments with unsustainable fiscal policies. They'll also short corporate and municipal bonds. They'll probably also short credit default swaps. Then they wait for their dire predictions to come true. The issuer runs into fiscal shortfalls. Alternatively, interest rates on their bonds could rise so high that they can't roll over their debt. Bond values plummet and the vigilantes clean up. Then they move on in search of the next issuer to hose.

When acting together, these institutional bond vigilantes can short a particular issuer *en masse*. This action erodes investor confidence and creates a tumultuous bond market. Everything falls.

Watch the media for word of the bond vigilantes and their activities. You will see massive selling in particular bonds—like they did with Greece and like they did with British Petroleum bonds during the Gulf Coast disaster. The vigilantes have the power to force governments and corporations to change their policies to those more to their liking. Bond vigilante actions can come suddenly. Their effects can be devastating.

China, in its insistence that the United States exhibit more fiscal responsibility, is just now beginning to express vigilante-like verbiage. If that verbiage turns into vigilante behavior, it will detonate the bond market nuclear explosion.

China sounds like any other investor worried about the stability of its bond issuer. At some point in the not-too-distant future, China will decide it no longer needs to recycle its trade balance surpluses into U.S. Treasury securities. We see this occurring when:

- Exports are less important to the Chinese economy because its middle class can finally afford homes, apartments, cars, and consumer goods and services.
- Domestic consumption becomes China's economic engine.
- China begins producing these consumer items internally in ever-increasing quantities. Quality rivals or exceeds that of any producer the world over.
- China's expanding economy will turn to buying domestic rather than foreign. This will leave discretionary investment funds in-country rather than sending them to the United States.
- Should China continue to see the United States behave in what it has said is a fiscally irresponsible manner, it will reduce the amount of U.S. Treasurys it buys until it is no more than a minor buyer. The United States will then have to try peddling its Treasurys elsewhere—at much higher rates.

Interpreting the Warning Signs

We chose just eight warning signs as our primary indicators of an imminent bond market collapse. There are many more. We felt each focuses on a particular bond market driver that is critical. Each is easily accessible in the mainstream media. Taken together, these eight warning signs provide adequate early warning of bond market problems.

Taken individually, no single sign means much. However, when you begin seeing a trend of five or more signs in the same direction, pay close attention.

If each is saying that there's a problem in its particular sector, then you should have general concern.

Most likely it is a concern not yet widely publicized. The trends of these indicators give you fair warning to take preemptive action before the masses beat you to it. From this advance warning alone, you will be far ahead of the game.

Moving into Chapter 2, "Manifestations of Nuclear Winter," you are now prepared to see how the gyrating interest rates and mounting bond defaults will affect your portfolio. We'll show you specific tactics and actions to take.

MANIFESTATIONS OF NUCLEAR WINTER

A fter seeing the warning signs of the bond bear market, people want to know what it will look like. What are some of the manifestations of the nuclear winter in Bondland? Listen to a conversation between El Greedo and his brother-in-law, Neo Fyte:

"Okay. I get that you're nervous about the family's bond portfolio."

"Nervous?" Greedo exclaimed. "Nervous is not the word, my sister's naïve spouse. Nervous happens when my sixteen-year-old daughter takes the BMW out to get gas. What I'm talking about is way beyond nervous."

"So what, then?"

"The bond market is headed for a nosedive—"

"I'm a visual person," Neo said, lost. "What's it going to look like?"

Greedo scratched his bearded chin. "Most people haven't a clue. No one knows when it's going to happen, either. It may be a matter of months; could be a year or more. My guess is that we'll probably have a few false starts before the bond market takes its big plunge. Some shallow dives, followed by recoveries. Just some expensive teases. Then—*wham*," Greedo smacked his palms together, "the big one hits and holds us down like a rogue wave crashing over our heads."

"But what're we going to see?"

"Never been one like the one that's coming, my inquisitive in-law. But here's what I think. First, interest rates climb. Rates will start rising faster and faster. Then we're going to see something happen with inflation or deflation—I don't know which. Probably inflation. Whatever, it'll be bad. These two things—interest rates rising and inflation or deflation movement—will cause cities to default on their bonds—"

"Bad news for us since our bond portfolio is about thirty percent bonds issued by cities. I checked."

Greedo eyed Neo with new interest. "So you did, my relative by marriage only. Municipal defaults are just the beginning, though. We're going to see something bigger. I think the U.S. is going to have a tougher and tougher time selling its Treasurys. As China, Japan, and the UK reduce their asset allocations to U.S. debt, America will start down an economic spiral—"

"A spiral that feeds on itself and gets worse the deeper it goes."

El's jaw partially dropped as he looked at Neo with a semblance of respect.

"What?" Neo asked. "I been readin'."

What Will Interest Rates Do?

El Greedo's comments above aren't too far off the mark. The 10-year Treasury pictured in Figure 2.1 shows how yields flashed up to 4 percent in April 2010 for just one day. This immediately dropped Treasury prices. The press heralded this as the long-awaited pullback for the bond market and a new fear of inflation gripped the media—*for just a few days*. Then yields came back down, prices rose to their old levels, and everything was fine once again.

The pundits would have you believe they know the exact direction interest rates will take. The truth is that no one knows. No question, interest rates have been in a downtrend since 1980. However, mixed in that trend are peaks and

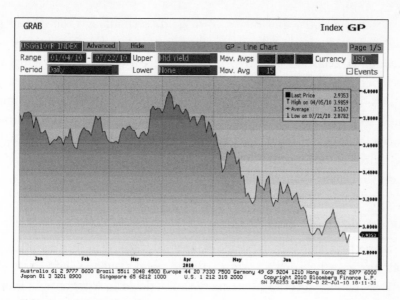

Figure 2.1   Ten-Year Treasury

Source: Bloomberg Finance LP. © 2010 Bloomberg Finance LP. All rights reserved. Used with permission.

valleys, some lasting a year or more. Who is to say that we won't experience a rapid spike in rates, as happened between 1976 and 1981? With rates at a generational low point as we go to print, the prudent investor's strategy is to plan on a rise in rates.

An upward change in interest rates will be both part of the cause and also the effect of the bond market's collapse. Rates may climb because the bond market and creditworthiness of the issuers is deteriorating. Investors demand to be compensated for the added risk they're taking. Watch for rising yields and plummeting bond prices. If you don't make preemptive changes, your portfolio value will fall with everyone else's. Read on. We're going to show you what to look for.

Characteristics of the Nuclear Winter

Watch for the general manifestation of what occurred during 2010: Gold prices and commodity prices of all types were at or near record highs. As the United States kept borrowing and printing money, as quantitative easing flooded the system with yet more money, emerging economies chastised the Fed. Their currencies were appreciating against the dollar, making it more expensive for other countries to buy their exports.

Watch the dollar and the price of gold. Even though the size of the gold market is not gigantic, if investors (Central Banks, institutions, *and* individuals) keep using gold as a surrogate currency, the emerging and developed countries will lash back. First, we'll see problems in the Treasury markets—higher yields and lower prices. The ripples created there will immediately spill over into the rest of the bond market. Use gold as an indicator of what the global markets think of our monetary and fiscal policies. Higher gold prices will cause the U.S. dollar to drop in value. This occurrence is deadly for bonds.

Changes in Yield Curve Shape

The causes for a change in the shape of the yield curve are numerous: inflation, economic growth, a debased currency, and bond vigilantes. Add to this list horrible Treasury auctions as an angry smack-down to irresponsible Federal deficits. All these causes taken separately or together can and will change the slope of the Treasury yield curve. It will go from positively sloped to an even more exaggerated positive slope. Long-term, intermediate-term, and short-term interest rates all will rise.

Back in 2009 and 2010, the banks that took TARP money repaid it as fast as they could. The government's terms and intervention in decisions that normally belonged to management alone were untenable to the banks. Instead, they hoarded cash and repaid the TARP money as soon as they could. The result was that, contrary to the government's intent, bank lending actually contracted. **Look for more bank lending as the bond market sinks.** Corporations and individuals will want to lock up loans as soon as they can for fear of rising interest rates and more expensive borrowing. Demand for commercial and industrial loans will also increase for the same reasons.

We anticipate that the yield curve will undergo transition. First, it will move from its normal positive slope, indicating a growing, healthy economy, to one that exemplifies a red-hot economy. As the bond market implodes, the yield curve will become more and more steeply sloped. Long-term Treasury bond yields will be hundreds of basis points higher than short-term Treasurys. Think of the Federal Reserve desperately trying to put the brakes on inflation. Think of a debased dollar the Fed must somehow prop up. All of this will manifest itself in the yield curve's steeply positive shape.

Lessons Learned from Greece

The vigilantes pummeled bonds in 2010 when they refused to buy any more Greek debt. The Greek government had to do something to entice bond buyers. So they increased yield. Even so, rolling over their debt at any cost proved impossible.

The Greek government and its lawmakers brought this debacle on themselves. They had created a *nanny state*—one that takes too much care of its citizens to the point they have little incentive to work and be productive. Nanny states simply cost too much. They don't produce the economic growth needed to sustain that level of governmental spending. It's just as former UK Prime Minister Margaret Thatcher so nicely characterized it: "The problem with socialism is that eventually you run out of other people's money to spend."

The Greek government feared bond holders wouldn't roll over their debt as it matured—essentially that they would get out of Greek bonds. The Greek government knew it couldn't afford to pay double-digit rates to entice bond buyers.

We can see how this played out in what it cost to insure Greek debt in the credit default swap (CDS) market. CDSs pay buyers if a borrower fails to meet its obligations. Suddenly, the price of Greek CDSs spiked as the market realized how expensive it was to buy insurance protection against a possible Greek default. The graph in Figure 2.2 illustrates the rise in the Greek CDS price.

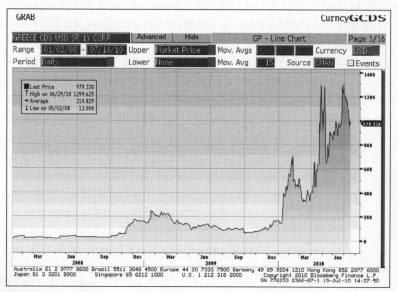

Figure 2.2   Greek CDSs

Source: Bloomberg Finance LP. © 2010 Bloomberg Finance LP. All rights reserved. Used with permission.

Greek Tragedy Hits Illinois

Illinois seems to have taken a page from Greece's troubles. By the summer of 2010, the state of Illinois had stopped paying its bills. The state owed $5 billion in current payables. Its cash coffers were empty. It desperately needed to issue bonds. It ended up issuing some bonds—just $900 million in Build America Bonds (BABs)—the proceeds from which, by statute, they could not use to pay bills.

Here's the disconnect: With the state in such financial disarray, wouldn't they need to "pay up" the interest rate on their BABs? Yes, but they didn't have to. Investors kept buying them, thinking that the federal government would bail out Illinois if something happened.

Did the Illinois lawmakers think that the same financial abyss Greece dived into couldn't happen to them? The truth is, like so many bond issuers, the elected officials tried to keep doing business the same way they have been doing it for the years leading up to their demise. After all, the old ways kept getting them reelected, which is all that matters, isn't it? Kicking the can down the road ran Illinois right into a dead end.

According to Bloomberg Financial, as we write this, 46 municipal bond issues defaulted during the first eight months of 2010. This totaled $1.7 billion. We see this as the precursor to the bond bear market. Many of these bonds were in Florida—the so-called *dirt bonds* that funded housing developments that never sold. With Florida, we expect to see significant bond defaults in California, Arizona, and Nevada.

Expect to see the bond bear market in munis begin to manifest itself in problems with nonessential service bonds. These are bonds issued to fund recreational facilities such as parks and professional sports stadiums and arenas. Library bonds are also discretionary, as are golf courses. An example is the Carter Plantation Community Development District in Louisiana, which missed a payment on its $23.5 million bond that funded development of its golf resort. Then there was Crawford, Indiana, that missed a payment on its $16.6 million bond sold to build a high-speed Internet system. The list gets longer by the month as the risks worsen.

ACTION STEP: NONESSENTIAL SERVICE BONDS

One of the first manifestations of the bond bear market will be shaky municipal finances and outright defaults of nonessential service bonds. Don't buy them. If you own them, sell them.

A Close Look

Both Greece and Illinois provide closeups of how the bond bear market manifests itself. States, counties, cities, and other municipalities are no different. They all become so financially strapped for cash that it will restrict their access to the capital markets. The bonds they sell will be so expensive for them to service that they will need to issue more and more bonds just to stay afloat. The more bonds they issue, the greater investors perceive the risk. The greater the risk, the higher the debt servicing cost to the municipality. It becomes a vicious cycle and cannot have a happy ending.

Another manifestation of the bond market's nuclear winter is a backlog of unpaid bills. The backlog will jump by huge percentages over relatively short periods. Again, Illinois is the poster child for how not to run state finances. Their backlog of unpaid bills in June 2009 was $2.8 billion—itself, not a small number. However, just one year later in June 2010, the same backlog of unpaid bills had soared to $5 billion. There was no end in sight. California is in similar dire fiscal straights. Several times they paid taxpayer refunds and vendors, not with checks that could be cashed, but with IOUs that couldn't.

As the nuclear winter approaches we will see Treasury auctions begin to experience the same inadequate participation as some state bond markets. High dependence on just a few mega-buyers—China, Japan, and the United Kingdom—will exacerbate the Treasury's problem.

China's anger over U.S. protectionism will grow more intense. As the 98-pound financial weakling, the United States continues its attempts to bully China's currency policies. It is clear that the U.S. Congress has no clue that it is China that holds the world's financial, currency, and trade surplus dominance—not the United States. In fact, the specifics are hiding in plain sight. As of the end of 2010, according to *Barron's* November 8, 2010 cover story, "China for the first time is investing more overseas in hard assets like copper, oil and iron, than in U.S. government bonds."

China clearly wants to redeploy its trade surpluses elsewhere. It makes no sense for them to buy U.S. government securities, just to see the currency erode. We think this is the start of something big.

Tail Risk

Think of the bell-shaped curve you may have learned about in statistics class (see Figure 2.3). It has two tails, one at either end. These are both on the outer reaches of its standard deviation.

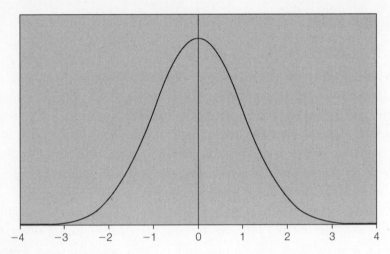

Figure 2.3   Bell-Shaped Curve

We're worried about the unlikely events at the two tails actually occurring—called *tail risk*. Bond investors are usually pretty good at managing their portfolios for events occurring around the center. But few people are any good at protecting themselves from the so-called *black swan events*—the unexpected, statistically rare events that occur at either tail.

■ ■ ■

"I don't know why they call 'em 'black swan events,'" complained El Greedo.

The brother-in-law, Neo, piped right up, "Actually, either end of the bell curve occurs only in statistically rare instances—on the outer fringes of the standard deviation—"

"So why name them after a bird?"

"Because they're so rare—like the occurrence of black swans. For centuries people thought only white swans existed. Then they discovered black ones in Australia in 1697."

El Greedo shook his head. "Your knowledge of irrelevant trivia always amazes me, my semi-relation."

■ ■ ■

Tail risk events are not unheard of. The fact is smart bond managers have been buying hedges against extreme market moves that most Wall Street financial models failed to detect since the 1980s. Three examples are:

1. The credit market meltdown and virtual bank insolvency in 2008–2009.
2. The collapse of Greece's sovereign debt in early 2010 that sent the euro to a four-year low against the U.S. dollar.
3. The 1,000-point flash-crash of the DJIA on a single day, May 6, 2010.

No model then in use predicted any of these events.

We anticipate outlier events manifesting themselves as any of these three occurrences:

1. Torturously high interest rates, making the bear markets of 1981 and 1994 seem like a picnic.
2. Depressed interest rates for an extended time, resembling Japan's experience. Though we don't expect this will happen, it certainly could.
3. Our elected officials on all levels suddenly becoming fiscally responsible and make the budget cuts necessary to compel America to live within its means, even if it means not getting reelected. Again, we don't think this will happen.

Any of these three qualify as a tail on the bell-shaped curve of unlikely events.

Impact on Municipalities

A serious manifestation of the nuclear winter strikes the bond issuers—mostly the overspending states, cities, and municipalities that depend on bonds to fund their cash requirements. What will happen to them if interest rates spike up and stay there for very long?

First, these smaller bond issuers may be unable to sell their new issues and get the money they need to operate—at any price. Investors' perception will be that the financial structure of these issuers is too fragile and risky. Investors demand compensation for the risk they take.

Issuers will default on their debt. They will stop paying their bills.

Bond issuers know that the capital markets will lock them out if they stiff their investors. Lawmakers will do everything they can to prevent it—short of doing something that may not get them reelected.

For small municipal revenue bond issuers without adequate backup from a stronger entity like the state, a default—even a technical one—may well mean that you won't get paid. Both Chicago and Cook County, Illinois, are examples of how this almost occurred. In 1932, both were on the verge of

ACTION STEP: DON'T PANIC JUST BECAUSE A BOND DEFAULTS

Yes, if you own a bond that defaults, you have a serious problem. Too many of these and your portfolio won't generate sufficient income on which to live. However, there are degrees of bond default. Just because a bond defaults doesn't necessarily mean you won't receive your interest or principal in the future.

Bonds can be in *technical* default of their indenture covenants for a variety of reasons: For corporates, perhaps the issuer failed to hit certain financial ratios; maybe they failed to submit financial statements on time. There are many more incidences of technical default. For munis, perhaps an issuer has used the last of its reserves. Certainly these events are not good news. But they may not actually impugn the issuer's ability to meet its bond payment obligations.

The fact is that bond defaults where the issuer actually failed to pay interest or principal are exceedingly rare for municipals. Since 1933, Arkansas is the only state that has failed to pay its bond holders and had to restructure its debt.

bankruptcy. They were behind in payroll for their municipal workers. Schools almost had to close because they hadn't paid the teachers for six months. Then, in a desperate attempt to avoid bond default, they asked for tax payments in advance of the due date from Commonwealth Edison, Illinois Bell, and several other substantial local companies. Chicago and Cook County used these proceeds to pay the $2.9 million due on their bonds. Let's hope history doesn't repeat itself anytime soon.

■ ■ ■

"So where do we stand with defaults in our portfolio?" asked Neo.

"None so far. But I heard about a small school district in central California."

"They're bankrupt?"

"No, my untested student. There's a big difference between default and bankruptcy. *Bankruptcy* means they don't have the money to pay their obligations and have to reorganize. Even then, bond holders will probably get paid. *Default* doesn't mean they can't pay. In this case, the school district just forgot to put the interest payment money into the proper disbursement account within three days of the payment date. The disbursing authority declared a technical default and issued a notice."

■ ■ ■

Even in bankruptcy there are ways to pay the bond holders. The most common way is to restructure the debt, perhaps by reducing the coupon to a more affordable level, at least until things turn around for the bond issuer. Maybe they'll extend the bond maturity if the municipality doesn't have the money to redeem maturing bonds and isn't confident it can float a new bond issue to cover the amount owed. There's almost always a way out of the mess the lawmakers create for their municipalities and to make bond holders whole short of declaring bankruptcy.

However, as the nuclear winter takes hold and the bond bear market unfolds, look for major issuers to do just that—declare either default or even bankruptcy.

In the corporate bond space, the federal government did the unthinkable to the General Motors bond holders in 2008. The Obama Administration forced bond holders into second secured position behind the UAW, which was never in the bankruptcy pecking order to begin with.

This action cost bond holders billions. The action was contrary to contract law. It was truly a once-in-a-lifetime event that no one could have ever anticipated occurring in a non-communist country.

Nevertheless, it appeared that the Obama Administration favored the autoworkers and their labor unions (comprising hundreds of thousands of voters) over the secured bond holders whose money had kept beleaguered GM afloat while management tried to hammer out a solution to their labor union problems. In case you missed it, we're pulling for the bond holders.

States Sell Assets

For Sale by Owner: Magnificent 432-acre site overlooking San Rafael Bay in beautiful Northern California. Comfortably houses 3,317 guests with expansion to 8,000 as needed. Exclusive guest list—by court appointment only. Views in some rooms, others enclosed. Fully occupied for over 150 years. Easy access to the Richmond/San Rafael Bridge. Gated community with unrivaled facilities for disposing of unwanted guests. On-site recreational facilities can be converted to a concert venue—previous performers include Johnny Cash.

The preceding is, of course, California's supermax San Quentin State Prison. Many states, counties, cities, and other municipal bond–issuing entities will have to sell assets just to survive. This is a bad omen for municipal bond holders.

Here are just a few of the municipal problems that we expect to lead the bond market meltdown:

Harrisburg, PA

Harrisburg, PA, had to beg its insurance company, Assured Guarantee Municipal Corp., to step up to make the interest payments on its $282 million incinerator debt. As a result it is selling all city-owned assets that aren't nailed down, including: the City Island and the sports facilities; the National War Museum and adjacent parking facilities; the water and sewage utility system; and city-owned Broad Street Market. If you own any bonds associated with these facilities, get out.

Georgia

The Peach Tree state was selling some of the loans it made to its cities for their water and sewer systems. These loans were low-hanging fruit and sold fairly quickly. This is just a very early manifestation of the bond bear market pain to come. Now that these easily sold assets are gone, what will Georgia do to raise the cash needed to pay for its budgetary excesses?

California

California, along with its famous prison, wants to sell the Los Angeles Memorial Coliseum. It probably won't happen since the site is a historical landmark— it's the only sports venue ever to host two Olympics—1932 and 1984. Selling it would be like selling the Statue of Liberty and allowing the new owners to rename it the Goldman Sachs Bronze.

Sale/Leaseback Deals for States

Desperate for cash, many states' problems will manifest themselves in slick financial deals designed to monetize non-revenue-producing assets. The first of these we expect to see are sale/leaseback deals for state-owned real estate. This deal monetizes the cash value just sitting there in state-owned real estate without giving up the right to use it. Some states will use the proceeds for specific programs such as jobs creation. Others will simply use it to pay current bills, forgetting about the next administration.

Once a sale/leaseback deal closes, the risk is that the state legislature must actually appropriate the funds needed each year. If they fail to appropriate these funds due to political infighting, then the deal will default. This will leave bond holders holding an empty bag.

If you own bonds issued by states or cities entering into such sale/leaseback arrangements, the first question you should ask is whether the legislature has

ACTION STEP: ASSET SALES

- Recognize that governmental asset sales are a symptom of extreme underlying fiscal distress.

- Review your portfolio and flag any bonds issued by government entities seeking to sell assets just to pay the bills. You may have to sell them as the bond market slides down the slope.

- Determine the stability of the payment stream for these questionable bonds—they shouldn't depend on the issuer selling assets to meet the bond debt. If you think they do, then get out.

- If you don't have a guaranteed payment stream such as refinanced bonds and bonds that are escrowed to maturity, then sell them.

already appropriated the lease service funds. If not, then the deal is at risk and will likely go south when the bond market crashes. The cash benefits to close these states' budget deficits will not likely be forthcoming. Lease-revenue bonds are lower in the bond pecking order to general obligation bonds.

Now that we know the warning signs of the coming bond bear market and now that we understand what it will look like, what do we do? Chapter 3, "Building Your Bond Fallout Shelter," describes what securities you need to move your portfolio into to survive the initial onslaught of the bond market crash.

BUILDING YOUR BOND FALLOUT SHELTER

Investment Vehicles That Work in a Bond Bear Market

"*Geez*, El, I feel a little panicky with all you're sayin' about a bond crisis and nuclear winter coming. Income from our investments goes to almost zip. The portfolio value drops like a rock. What're we going to do?"

"One thing we're not going to do is panic," said Greedo. "I made that mistake back in two-thousand-eight and nine. My stupid trades made things worse. Much worse."

"Yeah. You lost a million bucks!"

Greedo glowered at the reminder. "I'll make it back. This time slowly but surely without taking so much risk. Anyway, that was then. I know a lot more now. We're going about this in an organized way. Smart trades. Each with a specific purpose. We create a strategy to deal with this train-wreck that's coming around the next bend. A strategy that gets us through the worst of the nightmare and positions us to profit from the recovery when it finally comes."

■ ■ ■

El Greedo speaks the truth to his brother-in-law. Before the bond market's problems began in 2008, the Boomers were in the consumption phase of their lives. They weren't worrying obsessively about saving and adding to a retirement nest egg. They owned mostly stocks with some bonds sprinkled into the mix. Money market rates didn't make them rich but they were at least livable. Real estate was appreciating and saleable in a pinch. People didn't feel house-poor. Nest eggs had a certificate of deposit component with guaranteed double-digit returns. And there weren't as many fixed income funds as there are today.

Then the credit meltdown of 2008 and 2009 hit. It was awful—the worst in recent history. Before investors could pick themselves up off the ground, the sovereign debt crisis of 2009 through 2010 slammed them again.

The Baby Boomers had already suffered enough from their stock market losses. They attempted to reduce their risk exposure by shifting much of their investment money from stocks to bonds. Now, with more money in bonds and bond funds, we investors stand before the third crisis—the fall of America's corporate and public finance mechanism.

The bottom line is that there are now many more bond investors in a market that is about to tank. Notice in Figure 3.1 how the flow of funds stampeded into bond funds in 2009 without much letup in 2010.

When the bond market implodes, it will put a tremendous drag on the entire U.S. economy. Those investors with their money in bond funds will be

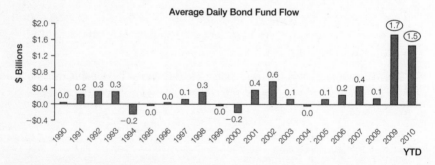

Figure 3.1 Flow of Bond Funds
Source: TrimTabs Investment Research © 2010. Used with permission.

among the most badly hurt. There's nothing worse than panic selling by an enormous crowd of panicked investors.

At least El Greedo has a frame of reference for what can happen to a bond portfolio during financial crisis. It seems his partner, Neo, has never had such a large part of his nest egg in fixed income instruments before. Given Neo's apparent inexperience, who wouldn't panic?

Pre-crash Asset Allocation

Some investors don't care if the value of their bond portfolio craters just as long as it still throws off coupon income. After all, that's what they're really after. We've heard the argument. It's easy to say this *before* the bond market crashes. Once it happens and investors see the value of their bonds falling 10 percent, even 20 percent, with each Federal Reserve interest rate hike, it's a different story.

Human nature is to panic when faced with such a dilemma. Panic begets panic and investors wonder: *With the value so far below what I bought it at, what happens if the issuer stops paying the coupon? Then, either I can't sell because no one will buy or I'll get just a fraction of what I paid. Then what?*

It's important to remember: The majority of bond and bond fund investors have never been through a protracted bond bear market. Certainly, many investors lived through the 2008 meltdown. The market bounced back. Investors who held on were mostly made whole. But the anticipated bond bear market, creating a nuclear winter, promises not to be so kind to bond investors. These are the same investors who had no skin in the game during the brutal bond bear markets of 1981 and 1994.

The potential for large-scale municipal bond default concerns those of us in the markets every day. Municipal finances are in a state of disarray and getting worse every day. Default and even the bankruptcy of some municipalities can and probably will happen. This whipsaw action of plummeting bond values *and* default on coupon payments will devastate investors who have failed to prepare their portfolios for this crash. Bond panic will feed on itself and create even greater losses in value.

Building a Fallout Shelter

Well before any bond market crash occurs, you need a safe haven for your investment portfolio. We call it a fallout shelter for your fixed income nest egg.

The intent is to replace ineffective bond structures with positions that will work for you in a bear market. This really isn't complicated. It just amounts to rebalancing your portfolio from whatever is in there now to the bonds needed to survive a severe bond market downturn.

Remember the tail risk—the event we see on the horizon could be either end of the tail—hyperinflation or deflation; interest rates spike or stay low with zero economic growth. We don't need to know the precise direction or the timing. If we're wrong on either, then the worst case is that you unnecessarily rebalanced your portfolio, took profits where you had them, harvested tax losses in other positions, and insulated your portfolio from something that didn't happen yet. We plan for the worst and hope for the best.

The first step is to determine your actual asset allocation—not just whether it's a corporate or a municipal bond, and not just whether it's a TIP, mortgage-backed, GNMA, or exchange-traded (ETF) bond fund. We need to go much deeper. We need to know all the other factors that create risk in a severely falling market.

ACTION STEP: USE YOUR AUTOMATED E-WORKBOOK

There is an automated e-workbook that accompanies this book. There is no extra cost for the e-workbook. You already own it with your purchase of this book. Access your e-workbook files using the special web site address and password in the appendix of this book. You'll download the Excel templates directly to your computer and do all of your work only on your computer. We did this to prevent any issues of security for your private, personal investment information.

We created the e-workbook as a simple Excel template. Most computers with the Microsoft Office suite already have Excel. Although your computer must have some version of Excel, you do not have to be familiar with Excel to use the e-workbook. We made it transparent and extraordinarily user-friendly. We hope you will use the e-workbook and see how clearly it portrays all of your fixed income allocations no matter how many different brokerage accounts or special-purpose portfolios you have.

We want you to aggregate your brokerage accounts. Look at them as a single consolidated account. The accompanying e-workbook makes consolidating your accounts across multiple trading platforms easy. The component asset allocations include:

- Corporate bonds:
  - By sector
- Municipal bonds:
  - By sector
  - By state
- Bond funds:
  - By type
  - By sector
- Government bonds:
  - By agency

Once you've identified the asset allocation of your bond portfolio, the e-workbook reports show you where your risk lies. For example, you may discover that you have corporate bonds with, say, an 85 percent concentration in corporate bonds issued by financial institutions. This undue concentration in a plummeting sector is what nuked so many during the 2008–2009 banking crisis. Or you may have 100 percent of your municipal bonds issued for nonessential services because they give higher yields. The *nonessential services*— municipal golf courses, sports stadiums, Internet facilities, and such—are often the first to default in a fixed income crisis, which we believe is just where America is headed.

Crash-Tested Investment Vehicles

In building a fixed income fallout shelter we want to take preemptive action that prepares for the worst. We don't want to stop at just creating a blast-resistant building. Instead, we want to furnish it with sufficient provisions to sustain us through the nuclear winter that follows.

Everyone has their favorite, can't-miss investment they swear can survive anything the economy throws at them. We've seen them all. Most fall sadly short of their hype. The problem is, by the time investors figure that out, it's too late. Here are the investment vehicles we believe belong in a fixed income portfolio *before* any bond market slump begins. They are tried and true. Nothing fancy or new here, but there is risk—you pay to play.

Constant Maturing Treasury (CMT) Bonds   If you go online looking for the definition of *constant maturity Treasurys*, you'll find two main entries:

1. The theoretical value of a U.S. Treasury is based on recent values of auctioned U.S. Treasurys.
2. The Federal Reserve calculates yields for "constant maturities" by interpolating points along a Treasury curve comprised of actively traded issues.

In plain English, there are bonds whose yields are calculated on specific CMT bonds. These are computed from a 1-year, 10-year, or other prearranged spot on the Treasury curve. Then, no matter how long you've owned the bond and how much time has passed, the yield earned is a percentage of the yield for that spot on the Treasury curve at the time coupon payment is due.

Another component of bonds based on the CMT is that they may have a prearranged coupon floor. If the yield on the constant maturing Treasury exceeds that floor, then bond holders receive a prearranged percentage of the constantly maturing Treasury yield. Does this sound complicated? Here's an example that will help.

Suppose you're building your bond fallout shelter and you chose the SLM Corporate bonds (CUSIP 78442FCT3). These are the old *Sallie Maes* with a CMT enhancement. The deal is that these bonds have a 4 percent coupon maturing on July 25, 2014. The 4 percent is the *floor*—the absolute least you'll receive. If the 10-year CMT exceeds the 4 percent floor, then you receive a prearranged percentage of the 10-year CMT at the time your coupon payment is due. In the case of SLM, that is 80 percent of the 10-year CMT. Should the yield on the 10-year CMT shoot up to 10 percent, then you will get an 8 percent yield (10% yield × 80% participation = 8% yield).

The beauty of CMT bonds is that some have a guaranteed floor while retaining a percentage of the upside. However, there is a risk.

The risk is that your bond issuer must not default on the bonds. Investors who buy bonds with CMT components knowingly trade interest rate risk for credit risk. Many CMTs are issued by banks and brokerage firms—the very sector that suffered so much in the 2008–2009 crash. Savvy investors using CMTs to help build their bond fallout shelters limit their asset allocations of these instruments to avoid excessive credit risk.

Fixed to Float   A nuclear winter for bonds in the form of higher rates will devastate the value of bond portfolios and bond funds. Many investors who stampeded into bond funds in 2009 and 2010 have never lived through a bear market in bonds. Worse still, investors' fixed income won't keep up with the resulting inflationary environment.

A partial antidote to this predicament is buying bonds whose coupon is fixed for a specific term, and then later floats over an index or specific rate. These bonds are called *fixed to float*. The bet is that interest rates will rise and the yield curve will steepen. We believe that's a pretty good bet.

Many financial institutions issue fixed-to-float bonds. Unfortunately, the majority of these are backed with derivatives. Their fixed coupons, indexes used, and percentage over the index paid all vary. Study the upside and the structure carefully so that you know exactly what you're getting.

As in all derivative-style securities, make sure you understand what you are buying. Ask specifically for fixed-to-float offerings and bonds linked to the 5- or 10-year CMT. If you buy in the secondary market, never, ever buy without consulting the latest TRACE system pricing on www.investingin bonds.com. This not only tells you where the bonds last traded but it also shows the trend over time. It will save you from being scalped by your broker.

ACTION STEP: CONTROLLED ALLOCATION

Your allocation of bonds linked to constant maturity Treasury and fixed-to-float bonds should be no more than 15 percent of your portfolio if they are all issued by financial institutions. If you include industrial issuers, then increase your allocation to 25 percent to include them as well. These are the bricks and mortar of your bond fallout shelter.

ACTION STEP: FIXED-TO-FLOAT EXAMPLES

General Electric Capital
Maturity: August 11, 2015, non-callable
Coupon: 2.50 percent to August 2011
Thereafter: three-month U.S. LIBOR + 75 basis points

Morgan Stanley
Maturity: July 28, 2017, non-callable
Coupon: 7.00 percent to July 2011
Thereafter: three-month U.S. LIBOR + 175 basis points

Morgan Stanley
Maturity: July 15, 2020, non-callable
Coupon: 7.00 percent to July 2012
Thereafter: three-month U.S. LIBOR + 200 basis points

Fannie Mae
Maturity: April 30, 2015, callable April 2012
Thereafter: three-month U.S. LIBOR + 65 basis points to April 2012
Thereafter: 4.00 percent if not called

If the teaser coupon appears too good to be true, it probably is. Either the structure is less than desirable; the amount issued is small; or something else is askew. Walk away.

Shorting Treasury Bonds in the Cash Market   Past bond bear markets have been bloody and savage. They have caused investors to swear that if they ever got out of their positions whole they would never buy bonds again. Hear a ring of familiarity? It should remind you of the equity bear markets of 2000 and 2007–2009. Stock investors uttered the same words. Look at them now.

If the nuclear winter brings ruinously high interest rates, then one strategy is to short Treasurys in the cash market. This is a strategy with a track record. Shorting Treasury bonds in the cash market provides a tried-and-true way to bet on higher interest rates while hedging your corporate and municipal bond portfolio.

Most brokerage firms require customers to short a minimum of $1 to $5 million in U.S. Treasurys. Additionally, you should know:

- Margin requirements vary depending on the brokerage firm and amount.
- You should only short Treasurys using the *repurchase agreement (repo)* market. Repo customers borrow the bonds from their brokerage firm and then sell them short. The interest rate you pay is the standard repo rate. This is the rate you want. **Do not do this transaction at the broker loan rate—you'll get skinned.**
- You must receive interest on the credit balance from the proceeds on your short sale. If your greedy broker refuses to pay on the credit balance, then don't do the trade with that broker.
- Remember, you are obligated to make coupon payments on the bonds you've borrowed. So, short the lowest-coupon Treasury bond you can borrow to limit the coupon payments you must pay. The price of the lowest-coupon Treasury bonds will decline the most. That is what you want.

  Alternatively, you may short long-term zero-coupon STRIPS (Separate Trading of Registered Interest and Principal of Securities). However, there's a caution here, too: STRIPS will be 25 percent more volatile. Leveraged, you can lose a lot of money if your timing is off and the Treasury market rallies. Even worse, your margin requirement will be larger due to additional market volatility. But if your timing is close to right, then shorting zero-coupon Treasurys will generate outsized profits.

Bond Futures When bond professionals short the Treasury market they usually use *interest rate futures*. These trade on the Chicago Board of Trade (CBOT; merged with the CME; now called the CME Group). This entity offers futures contracts on 2-year, 5-year, 10-year, 15-year, and 30-year U.S. Treasury notes and bonds.

The good news is that this is a huge and very liquid market. The bad news is that the market can quickly go against you. This misdirection can be hazardous to your financial health.

There is no higher high than making a quick leveraged score in the futures market. The counter to that comes when the market goes against you. Then you are subject to relentless margin calls that can quickly become financially crippling. Timing is everything when trading futures. You may be right on the direction of bond prices and yields. But if your timing is not spot-on or your margin account cash reserves are inadequate, you can go broke. That is why we don't recommend trading bond futures for investors or their brokers who are not experienced in this specific area.

Options on Futures   Most seasoned investors are familiar with the options market. A safer way to bet on higher interest rates or lower Treasury bond prices is the options market.

Tons of institutions use puts on Treasury bond futures for insurance. Buying puts is the safest way of minimizing your loss if rates go against you. By buying puts on Treasury bond futures, the most you can lose is the premium you paid.

Selling options on futures can be tricky. We recommend that only those already familiar with the futures and options market use it to build their bond fallout shelter. Unlike the inverse-leveraged Treasury ETFs, options and futures have been around for decades. They have proven themselves through multiple bear markets—if you know what you're doing.

Educate yourself. Practice on paper before you initiate a position. There's a reason why the CBOT's disclaimer appears all over their advertisements and marketing literature.

LEAPS   A subset of interest rate options is *LEAPS* (long-term equity anticipation securities). These are options on the *yield* of U.S. Treasury securities. They represent short-, medium-, and long-term rates. A call buyer anticipates rising interest rates. LEAPS and inverse Treasury ETFs (detailed in Chapter 5) provide a strategy for sheltering and hedging bond portfolios during the bond nuclear winter. Study them. Decide which ones meet your risk tolerance and then execute.

Building blocks for your fallout shelter consist of bricks, mortar, rebar, and lumber for the frame. Populating your portfolio with bonds that have fixed-to-float coupons based on the CMT formula, short Treasury ETFs, options on futures, and LEAPS on Treasury bonds are all possible choices to survive the bond market's nuclear winter. Doing nothing ensures you of a low probability of portfolio survival.

Making Duration Work for You

The *duration* of a bond is simply a measure of its sensitivity to a change in interest rates. We measure duration in years. For example, say a bond portfolio has an average duration of 5. This means that if interest rates go up just 1 percent, the value of that bond portfolio will *decrease* by approximately 5 percent. The converse is also true: If interest rates fall by 1 percent, the portfolio value will rise by about 5 percent. It is not a linear relationship due to the phenomenon of *convexity*. Convexity (as the quants call it) is the second derivative of how bond prices vary with interest rate moves.

The computation of duration is fairly involved. We do it all for you in the accompanying automated e-workbook. The e-workbook calculates duration for every bond you input and then computes the average weighted duration for the portfolio taken as a whole. Duration is not a static number like yield-to-maturity. The duration of a bond changes over time.

Since we anticipate interest rates to rise significantly in the future, we would naturally want a bond portfolio with a short duration. That way, as interest rates ratchet up, the value of our bond portfolio doesn't suffer nearly as much.

A short-duration bond portfolio becomes less and less sensitive to movements in interest rates as it rolls down the yield curve (that is, as the positions get closer to maturity). Short duration is a great way to keep your powder dry (prevent portfolio value erosion). So when the green shoots of bond market recovery appear, you're in position to pounce on new opportunities.

ACTION STEP: IDENTIFY A MAXIMUM DURATION YOU CAN LIVE WITH

Establish a maximum average duration for your rebalanced bond portfolio before the unthinkable occurs and the bond market suffers a catastrophic crash. This should be a percentage loss that you can live with if rates go up. Since we anticipate interest rates to rise, we recommend a short average duration of no more than four years.

Use the automated e-workbook to compute average duration for your portfolio. Adjust your bond holdings until you reach a maximum duration of 4. This means you may have to sell some positions whose durations are too long and represent a significant part of your portfolio. The automated e-workbook makes this *what-if* analysis a snap.

Rebalancing Before the Crash

Before the bond market crashes, there is some rebalancing of your portfolio that will insulate it and cushion the shock of the downward plunge. Figure 3.2 illustrates the asset allocation to use before the bond market tanks.

Having a constant maturing Treasury (CMT) component and fixed-to-float bonds provides a good minimum yield no matter how slowly or rapidly interest rates rise. If rates shoot up—as many, including ourselves, believe will happen—then they preserve your capital. By allocating 15 percent of the portfolio to CMTs and fixed-to-float bonds, you keep your options open before the crash occurs.

We recommend 30 percent of the portfolio be allocated to:

- ETFs that are short Treasurys
- LEAPS

This allocation provides most investors the means to take advantage of upward momentum in interest rates. As rates rise, so will the value of this segment of the portfolio.

The other 30 percent allocation is more conservative. It includes a laddered bond portfolio with a maximum duration of four years. You may substitute short-duration bond funds for part of or for the entire laddered bond portfolio. The accompanying e-workbook computes duration by individual bond and for your entire bond portfolio. Since the duration is short, if rates rise rapidly, the laddered bonds will limit your loss in value. Do not include in this segment any TIPS (Treasury inflation protected securities) or zero-coupon bonds.

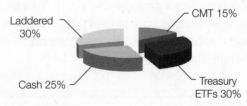

Figure 3.2   Pre-crash Allocations

The final 25 percent allocation goes to cash. Consider it *ready money* that you may allocate to opportunities as they become apparent throughout the bond bear market.

If you follow these recommendations, your bond portfolio will be as insulated from a bear market as you can make it. However, your openness to other points of view needs testing. Chapter 4, "Deflation," shows what else could happen and how to respond.

Chapter 4

DEFLATION: A POSSIBLE CRACK IN THE FALLOUT SHELTER

"You seem so hell-bent on protecting us from rampant inflation—"

"I am," said El Greedo. "With America's massive debt load I just don't see any other way the economy can turn but toward inflation and rising interest rates."

Neo studied his mentor for a second. "Okay. I don't disagree with you. But I'm just sayin', what if you're wrong? What if, somehow, some way we find ourselves in a deflationary environment like Japan? It could happen."

■ ■ ■

By now it's no secret that we agree with Greedo. We don't believe deflation is as much a likelihood as interest-rate-fueled inflation. We view an extended deflationary spiral as a tail-risk event—something out on the tail of the bell curve. Sure, it could happen. So, being prudent investors who are also watchful and open minded, we're going to allocate a portion of the fallout shelter portfolio to insulate you from deflation, should it happen.

We'll watch it carefully. If it looks like the pendulum has swung toward the deflation scenario, we'll allocate a larger portion to our deflation-advantaged securities. We do that out of an abundance of caution even though we *think* the probability of deflation actually occurring for a lengthy time is lower than the probability of inflation.

The Case for Deflation

The last real deflation scare for the U.S. economy occurred way back in 2000–2003, right as the dot-com bubble was bursting. Turns out the scare was a reaction to the dot-com companies that imploded. Their values tanked. People saw the value of the stocks they held in these companies drop like a stone. They panicked and cried "deflation."

What actually happened was investment money scurried from stocks to real estate, commodities, and even art. Prices in these areas began soaring—hardly deflationary.

The well-developed U.S. economy has been *deleveraging*—reducing its debt—since the end of 2008. Our government is reregulating in a big way. The boys at PIMCO, the world's largest bond fund manager with over $1.24 trillion under management, say we're experiencing *deglobalization*—the process of diminishing interdependence and integration between independent nation-states. Still, the specter of deflation remains a risk as the bond market barrels toward the edge of the cliff and the nuclear winter looms just over the horizon.

Some may welcome deflation. After all, the things they buy become less expensive. Think again. Deflation is not a good thing. It erodes profits and asset values. People avoid spending because they fear whatever they buy today will be cheaper tomorrow. The psychology of deflation feeds on itself. Deflation creates a downward spiral of lower profits. Here's how it works: Deflation:

- Causes companies to cut expenses, which . . .
- Stops expansion and hiring dead in its tracks, which . . .

- Reduces the workforce by layoffs, furloughs, and reduced work weeks, which . . .
- Creates a loss of consumer confidence since people are afraid for their jobs, which . . .
- Reduces consumer spending, which . . .
- Drives prices down further, which . . .
- Creates even more deflationary pressure and sends us right back to the beginning of this list.

Flow of Capital

Investment capital flowing from developed countries like the United States into emerging market countries like China and India is causing an inflationary bubble for assets in the emerging markets and lower prices in the United States and other already-developed countries.

Financial seers employ the *Weekly Leading Index*, published by the Economic Cycle Research Institute, as an indicator of future U.S. economic growth. Yes, we keep an eye on the *Weekly Leading Index*. If this index's annualized growth rate goes negative, it is supposed to indicate recession. Usually, with a severe, prolonged recession comes disinflation.

Along with the *Weekly Leading Index*, the Philadelphia Federal Reserve Bank's *Business Activity Index* is often touted as a recessionary predictor. To those who fear deflation, if both of these two respected indexes head in the same negative direction, they will build a case for deflation.

Deflation and the National Debt

With America's huge national debt, deflation is the last thing our government wants. Deflation would force the United States to repay its national debt in more valuable dollars. Naturally, there's no way our federal government wants that to happen. The Fed prefers to repay its debt from a *normally* inflated economy using *less valuable* dollars.

The Fed has the tools to ensure this scenario. It can buy Treasurys and mortgage-backed securities to quell deflationary pressures. Indeed, the U.S. government can encourage inflation. By itself, this is a powerful weapon to dampen deflationary tendencies.

Another Lesson from Greece

There are some similarities and some differences between the financial catastrophe we saw occur in Greece and the problems America faces. The bailout funds between the two countries are not even close in size. The European Union cobbled together a rescue loan package worth only $145 billion for Greece. By comparison, with estimates ranging everywhere from $500 billion to over $8 trillion, the cost of the U.S. bailout for its financial institutions dwarfs Greece's by a huge margin.

The point is what both countries have done about it.

Bailout Repayment Plans: Greece versus United States

Greece	United States
Raised taxes	Also raised taxes
Cut the wages of public employees	Also cut the wages of some public employees
Levied new taxes on luxury real estate properties	Added new taxes to the wealthiest Americans
Wants to show voters that the wealthy are footing the bailout bill	Ditto
Real estate values have plummeted	Jury is still out on inflation versus deflation

Combating Deflation

"You're askin' me what we should do in the unlikely event deflation hits? That's what you're askin'? Because if you really want to know the truth, I haven't a clue."

Neo jumped at the chance. "I do—"

"You?" Greedo asked. "You know how to insulate our bond fallout shelter from deflation?"

"It's common sense, my self-confident relation. I'd allocate some fixed income investments that won't go down in value as prices fall. I'd move us into higher quality bonds. Above all, the issuer must stay solvent in order to pay our coupon interest and principal. But of course, you are the captain of this ship."

"How do you know this, my increasingly educated brother-in-law?" asked Greedo.

"I subscribe to *Marilyn Cohen's Bond Smart Investor* newsletter," answered Neo. "If you want a free three-month trial subscription, just go to www.newsletters .forbes.com/SurvivingTheBondBearMarket, then follow the directions."

■ ■ ■

Neo is learning both about investments and how to handle Greedo's ego. Should the U.S. economy enter a deflationary cycle, investors will need a reliable income stream that does not fall with interest rates or prices. That means allocating a portion of the portfolio to high-quality fixed income securities. Here's our shopping list:

- Corporate bonds—investment grade, BBB or better.
- Municipal bonds that are prerefunded and escrowed to maturity. These bonds cannot default unless the Treasury repudiates our debt—which won't happen.
- Essential service revenue bonds that issuers probably won't default on because people need the water and sewers for their towns that these instruments fund.
- Solid bond issues with strong balance sheets, substantial cash flow, and plenty of money in reserve accounts to weather the coming storm. Avoid highly leveraged companies.
- Treasurys, especially long-term Treasurys. To combat deflation we want to *lengthen* duration. The object is to keep that higher fixed income rate going through the deflation cycle.
- iShares 20-year Treasury bond exchange-traded fund (TLT).
- STRIPS: These are zero-coupon Treasurys. Their fixed interest rates are locked in *and* the income is automatically reinvested.
- Federally guaranteed bank CDs.
- Bond funds but with longer durations.
- Cash: There's nothing wrong with holding cash in a deflationary environment even though it returns zero. If deflation were to take hold, cash gains in value as prices fall. Cash holdings allow investors to pick off targets of opportunity as they surface.

If you believe there is a real risk of deflation, then you want to avoid TIPS (Treasury inflation protected securities) and iBonds (inflation-linked savings bonds). These two will surely lose value should deflation take hold.

Allocating for Deflation

It makes sense to allocate a percentage of your bond fallout shelter to strategic deflationary securities. Your allocation percentage should reflect how strongly you believe deflation could occur. For example, if you think there's a 10 percent chance of deflation occurring, then allocate roughly 10 percent to deflation-advantaged securities.

You can always change the deflationary allocation once the bond bear market hits and we get a better sense of the inflation/deflation direction.

The Best Deflation Trade

In bond investing, as in life, timing is everything. Should the deflationary forces begin to swell, the most profitable bond trade is to buy zero-coupon long-term Treasury STRIPS—but only for those who can take the risk. For those who prefer to avoid such a gamble, buy long-term U.S. Treasury bonds that pay coupons.

The difference is the volatility a zero has versus a coupon-paying Treasury. Study these two revealing Bloomberg screens in Figures 4.1 and 4.2. One is for the risky zero; the other is for the more conservative coupon-paying Treasury. These are Total Return Analyses showing six "what-if" interest rate scenarios. The what-ifs delineate 50, 100, and 150 basis points interest rate shifts, both up and down.

If an investor purchased a 30-year Treasury bond with a 4.375 percent coupon yielding 4 percent and rates rise 150 basis points, the price plunges from 106 11/32 to 83.621 for a total negative return of −37.89 percent. But if deflation ravages our economy and rates instead *fall* 150 basis points, this same 30-year bond price rises to 138.54 for a +63.52 percent total return (including price appreciation as well as coupon payments).

Compare this to the more aggressive deflation trade: Buying long-term zero-coupon Treasury STRIPS. In this case, the 30-year STRIPS purchase price is 28.404 for a 4.35 percent yield to maturity. Should rates rise 150 basis points, the price plummets to 19.00 for a −65.37 percent total negative return.

However, should deflation hit, these zeros are the brass ring. If interest rates instead decline by 150 basis points, the zeros you paid 28.404 for are now priced at 44.34 for a +111.13 percent total return.

If you have a mathematically oriented view, notice that the price appreciation and price depreciation does not follow a linear path. That's because

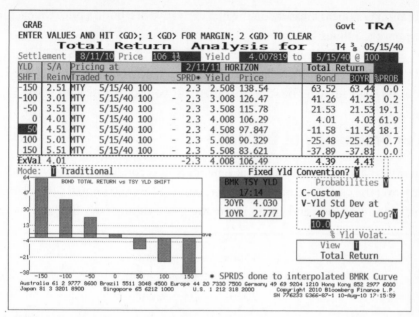

Figure 4.1   Thirty-Year Coupon-Paying Treasury

Source: Bloomberg Finance LP. © 2010 Bloomberg Finance LP. All rights reserved. Used with permission.

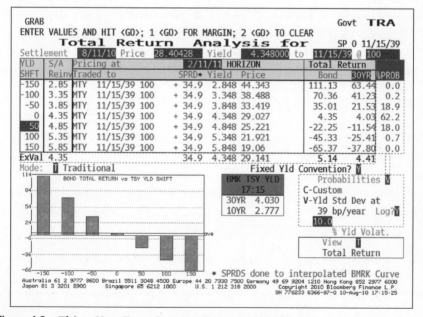

Figure 4.2   Thirty-Year Zero-Coupon Treasury STRIPS

Source: Bloomberg Finance LP. © 2010 Bloomberg Finance LP. All rights reserved. Used with permission.

duration is a linear measure on the first derivative of a bond's price changes in response to interest rate moves.

The bottom line is this: Prices on zero-coupon Treasury STRIPS are *far* more volatile. Hence we've dubbed them the *ultimate deflation trade*. However, your timing had better be spot-on; otherwise, you could lose your shirt.

The Probability of Deflation

David Zervos, respected analyst at Jefferies & Co., conducted a study of inflation over the past 50 years. Here are his computed average annual CPI inflation rates (omitting food and energy) from the 1960s through the 2000s:

1960s: 2.53 percent
1980s: 5.22 percent
1990s: 2.93 percent
2000s: 2.54 percent

Yes, the rate of inflation has been falling since the 1980s. Still, it *is* inflation. We believe that there certainly exists the potential for deflation to occur. However, the probability is far more likely that we'll experience either significant inflation as the result of rising interest rates, reemployment, and a recovering economy, or at least an inflation-neutral scenario.

Chapter 5, "Bond Funds," provides the insight you'll need to determine when to exit this popular investment vehicle that has by now run its course.

BOND FUNDS: SELL TODAY AND WALK AWAY

When the Boat Is Sinking Faster Than You Can Bail

Recall the dot-com era that ended in May 2000. Right up until the end, investors kept throwing money into any Internet-related startup and the private equity funds that threw gasoline on the dot-com fire. The same thing happened in 2009–2010 with bond funds. There was a massive rebalancing of money *from* equities and equity funds and *into* bond funds. Most of this money went into taxable bond funds.

■ ■ ■

"Why should we care about the flow of funds?" asked Neo.

Greedo said, "You're a student of history. It should make sense to you that history says when too much money floods a single asset class, the party is over."

"So what's the smart money do, brother of my wife?"

■ ■ ■

Our earlier book, *Bonds Now!*, anticipated the massive movement of money from stocks and stock funds to bonds and bond funds. But that was not the smart money. It was just the herd moving itself to greener pastures. The really smart money already noticed the herd stampeding into bond funds at weekly rates exceeding $4 billion. Figure 5.1 shows that the herd actually started its stampede in December 2008.

By the end of 2010, the cash inflows to bond funds hadn't let up. Indeed, even as we write this, bond funds are receiving more money each week than ever. PIMCO, the largest bond fund manager with about $1.24 trillion under management, gets a weekly shipment of about $1 billion in fresh cash flooding into its coffers. How long can so many people with so much money be right? Answer: They can't be right forever. The smart money knows its forever has ended.

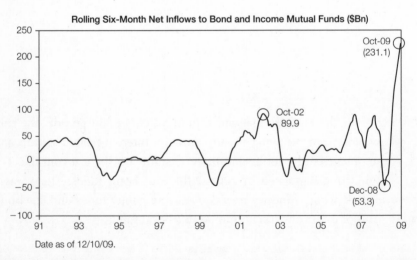

Figure 5.1   Bond Fund Cash Inflows
Source: Investment Company Institute and Morgan Stanley Investment Management. Used with permission.

Why the Move to Bond Funds?

It's always easier to allow the current of popular opinion to sweep you along. Investors want to trust that so many people—some of them supposedly the smartest investors on Wall Street—couldn't possibly be wrong. Nevertheless, just like the feeder funds that enabled Bernie Madoff's Ponzi scheme, they are wrong.

The smart money looks ahead to the implications of such a massive inflow. First, with so much money flowing into bond funds—and most of it flowing into taxable bond funds at that—what happens to bond prices?

Good question. There is so much money in these bond funds that managers must deploy it any way they can. This created such competition in both corporate and municipal bonds that prices rose and yields fell. Combine that with investors' preference for the safety of a bond. Even though average bond yields in these funds have fallen, the fund price is still up there due to excessive demand.

A startling example was in mid-2010, when investors in companies like Verizon, Altria, and Bristol Meyers Squibb could earn more on the dividend of their stocks than on the yield of their 10-year corporate bonds. Nevertheless, they bought the bonds and the bond funds that held them because investors perceived these as safer than the same company's stock. After all, the real estate market was still depressed and cash accounts earned just about 1 basis point yield, basically nothing. Bond funds offered a safe alternative that actually paid a return.

When money is flowing into bond funds with the ferocity of a wide-open fire hose, managers must *pay up* for the bonds they're buying—pay a higher price than they normally would. This eventually drives fund distributions and dividends down.

The Fallacy of Diversification

Many investors sought comfort that their new bond funds were diversified because the fund held lots of different bonds. The fund price went up because interest rates fell and demand for bond funds was insatiable. Everyone wanted in. The total returns on bond funds were great but they couldn't keep going in one direction forever. Here's how El Greedo learned this lesson:

■ ■ ■

"We're diversified, aren't we?" asked Neo. "I mean this bond fund we're in holds a raft of different bonds. All munis, sure, but they're from different issuers. We're okay, right?"

El Greedo remembered the same error he made a few years ago. "No. We're not okay, my fledgling assistant money manager. I once thought I was diversified because I owned Citi, Morgan, Chase, BofA, GMAC, and a host of other big banks. For all the good it did me I may as well have stuck all my money in just one of those names—"

"Sounds diversified to me. What happened?"

Greedo said, "They weren't diversified in industry or asset class. Not even the GMACs—that was just a financial institution in drag. When the shit storm hit the financial markets in oh-eight, it took every one of my financial institution holdings down with it."

■ ■ ■

Take no comfort from holding several different bond funds. Even though they hold a diversified portfolio, they're the same asset class—*a Treasury, a corporate, or a municipal bond fund—just different bond sectors*. When the bond market implodes, investors in each of these bond funds will stampede out. Prices will plummet. So much for the safety of diversification that comes from holding several bond funds. At the end of the day, they're all still the same asset class—bond funds.

There have been three historic mass movements to favored asset classes:

1. Tech stocks and tech funds in the 1990s. Most investors lost their shirts beginning in 2000.
2. Real estate, beginning in 2000–2003. This formed the real estate bubble that finally burst in 2007–2009. Real estate investors got hosed.
3. Bond funds, beginning in 2009. The jury is still out as to when (not *if*) these investors will realize that the music stopped while they were still on the dance floor.

With so much new money to deploy, the bond funds are competing among themselves. This competition drives down the interest that issuers must pay to float their bonds.

Let's examine the poor (and we do mean *poor*) state of California. The Golden State has severe budget problems—a $24 billion deficit. Its credit metrics keep deteriorating. But once again, the rating agencies haven't the guts to downgrade California. Still, after signing its budget, California quite successfully issued *general obligation* bonds. Excessive demand for municipal bonds from large institutions, including bond funds as well as retail investors, helped California successfully float its issue at an even more favorable interest rate.

At the beginning of the fourth quarter 2010, the disconnect between California's (substitute Illinois', New York's, Los Angeles's, or others') horrific finances and its limbo low yields made no sense. Investors' mindset was that if there were a large default, then the federal government would come to the rescue. Bailout mentality was the only explanation when investors were buying five-year California general obligation municipal bonds at a 1.65 percent yield to maturity.

The Risk of Staying in Bond Funds

The time to get out of any investment is when everybody wants in. It's the contrarian's old saw: *I'm a seller when everyone else is a buyer.* Or, if you've ever been on the noisy trading floor, they say, "When they're yellin' you should be sellin'."

When investment values are falling—as may bond funds in a rising interest rate environment—time seems to accelerate. Investment values usually fall much faster than they rise. It's the same with bond funds when they fall off the cliff. The same thing happened in November and December 2008. Remember the pain.

Much of the new money coming into bond funds in 2009 was money investors transferred from their stock holdings. They were inexperienced in the bond market. Many had just owned CDs and money market funds their entire lives.

Foretelling the Bond Fund Meltdown

We see three ways the market can go for bond funds:

1. The economic recovery stalls and the feared double-dip recession tightens its grip.
2. The economy simply slogs along sideways, not deteriorating any further, but not really picking up any appreciable growth, either.
3. Interest rates spike upward.

Scenario #1: The Economy Dies Should this happen, expect interest rates to fall below what they are now. This drives bond prices up. The net asset value (NAV) in bond funds would naturally increase. However, their dividend payments must inevitably fall, and fall hard. This is because the bond fund must deploy all that new money flowing into its coffers at tomorrow's significantly lower yields. The rising bond fund price due to excess demand cannot keep pace with the lower yields fund managers must accept when deploying all that new money.

The bond fund managers will have no choice but to lower their payouts. Novice bond fund investors will become confused. They'll see the value of their holding rise, but fail to understand why they aren't receiving a commensurately increased payout.

There's another problem for bond funds. Even the supposedly high-quality bonds in their portfolios may encounter financial difficulty as the economy rolls over and dies. We anticipate that if the economy dives into another recession, the bond market—especially the municipal bond market—will experience some significant defaults. Suddenly bond fund investors who thought they were insulated from such things not only have interest rate risk, but they also have credit risk to worry about.

Scenario #2: The Economy Slides Sideways If the economy fails to improve, but doesn't go down much further, this will keep interest rates moving in a tight trading range. Bond funds maintain a constant return over a diversified portfolio. We expect their prices to keep rising since people would continue throwing in more money. For bond fund investors, this isn't such a bad place to be—except for the fact that yields and distributions decline.

Scenario #3: Interest Rates Spike What happens if something causes rates to spike? The cause could be a sharp upturn in the economy, consecutive bad Treasury auctions, or significant municipal defaults. Perhaps a big city like Los Angeles or New York defaults.

This would produce an immediate decline in the value of bond funds. There would be a mass exodus, further depressing bond fund net asset values. Fund managers would have to sell their bonds for whatever they could get to raise cash to pay their investors demanding their money back. This time it will be worse. Dumping such a massive amount of bonds on the market all at once would further depress bond values. Bond fund investors would lose their shirts.

Which Bond Funds to Buy

We understand that bond fund investors are reluctant to give up their holdings in favor of buying the individual bonds. For one thing, bond funds are fast and relatively easy to buy. Investors don't have to do the research the bond fund managers would do (or should do) if they were buying individual bonds.

Then there's the argument for diversification. We can't argue with that—except to remind you that bond funds will get crunched in two of the three scenarios above.

Investors who insist on owning bond funds rather than the individual bonds should chose carefully. We have several that we think are safe to hold in the coming nuclear winter.

Going Long the U.S. Treasury Bond

There is an exchange-traded fund (ETF) that goes by the ticker symbol *TLT*. It is run by Blackrock Fund Advisors. TLT generally corresponds to the price and yield performance of the Barclays Capital U.S. 20+ Year Treasury Bond index. The fund invests about 90 percent in the bonds of the underlying index and at least 95 percent of assets in U.S. Treasurys. Its charter also allows it to invest up to 10 percent of its assets in U.S. government bonds not included in the underlying index. About 5 percent of its assets can go to repurchase agreements collateralized by U.S. government obligations and in cash and cash equivalents. At 0.15 percent, TLT's expense ratio is about half the category's average.

Since TLT is an exchange-traded fund rather than an open-end bond fund, investors can exit without any difficulty. This ETF will perform in a noninflationary or deflationary environment. However, should interest rates suddenly rise, the price will plummet. TLT would not be the right ETF to own in that case.

Table 5.1 Inverse Bond ETFs

Symbol	Name	Market Cap*	Avg. Volume	200 EMA
TBT	ProShares UltraShort 20+ Year	$4,210.49	8,415,060	$42.80
TBF	ProShares Short 20+ Year Treas	$437.22	199,084	$46.70
PST	ProShares UltraShort 7-10 Year	$336.35	120,870	$48.42
TMV	Direxion Daily 30 Yr Trsy Bear	$153.66	283,094	$55.37
TYO	Direxion Daily 10 Yr Trsy Bear	$41.41	14,802	$55.72
TWOZ	Direxion Daily 2 Yr Trsy Bear	$9.61	7,379	$39.43
SBND	PowerShares DB 3x Sht 25+ Yr T	$4.66	1.570	$23.38
FLAT	iPath US Treasury Flattener ET	$4.12	24,217	$50.30
DTUS	iPath US Treasury 2-year Bear	$4.01	3,100	$50.17
DTYS	iPath US Treasury 10-year Bear	$3.89	5,821	$50.09
DLBS	iPath US Treasury Long Bond Be	$3.86	3,094	$49.85

*Market Cap is shown in millions of dollars.
Source: ETFdb © 2010. All rights reserved. Used with permission.

Shorting the Market with Inverse Bond ETFs

As the bond market begins to implode a number of alternatives exist to either reduce your losses or actually take advantage of the downward direction. Inverse ETFs provide a way to short the bond market. Table 5.1 lists some of the more common inverse bond ETFs.

By allocating a segment of your bond portfolio to inverse bond ETFs, you limit downside risk. An advantage of using an ETF to provide insurance against rising interest rates is that your maximum loss is capped at your original investment value. Other methods of shorting the markets expose investors to unlimited losses if their timing is off and the market runs away from them.

The Biggest Bond Funds

We don't mean to show any disrespect to the large, well-run bond funds. They have had an admirable 30-year run. Nevertheless, we believe the party is winding down. Here are some of the most successful:

PIMCO Total Return (PTTRX)

PIMCO markets its Total Return fund as a diversified portfolio of high-quality bonds. They actively manage the portfolio with the intent of maximizing returns while controlling investor risk. This particular fund values consistent performance. It achieves this by taking modest risk in its various fixed income investment categories. Such a strategy reduces the risk of poor performance due to any single allocation category cratering. However, such a strategy also reduces the upside.

PIMCO allocates a majority (about 63 percent) of its Total Return fund to government-related instruments. With effective duration at about five years, this fund responds modestly to changes in interest rates. This fund can invest in securities most individual investors can't do on their own—like credit default swaps, futures, options on futures, and LEAPS. All of PIMCO's investments are in large trades at commission levels that individual investors cannot match.

Loomis Sayles Bond Fund (LSBRX)

Loomis Sayles is a high total investment return fund, seeking current income and capital appreciation. About 80 percent of the fund is in fixed income securities. Of this, up to 35 percent goes into lower-rated bonds and about 20 percent is in preferred stocks. The fund may invest in fixed income securities of any maturity. Minimum investment is $2,500. With a significant part of the fund in lower-rated bonds, we see this fund as slightly more risky. However, its returns should compensate for that risk.

Vanguard GNMA Fund (VFIIX)

We suggest entering the Vanguard GNMA fund after interest rates finish their rise and begin leveling off. This fund had a great 20-year run. However, it will not perform well in a rising interest rate and rising mortgage rate environment.

Deciding to Exit Bond Funds

Get out of bond funds when you notice interest rates start to climb. That's not an easy thing to do. We've had a lot of false starts over the years. However, knowing what indicators telegraph a coming move in interest rates isn't all

ACTION STEP: SELLING BOND FUNDS

Don't sell your funds all at once. Sell a piece and invest the proceeds in individual bonds with final maturities. Then sell another chunk, then another hunk, always with the proceeds immediately reinvested. Populate the portfolio with a diversified collection of individual bonds that meet your income needs.

that difficult. Chapter 1, "Warning Signs," identified a number of them. Yet, believing what you see, and then having the courage of your convictions to actually execute the indicated trade, is often something else entirely.

Indicators and Direction

Begin liquidating your bond fund holdings when you see the key indicators change to a consistent direction. Follow the same indicators we first introduced in Chapter 1. What is good for the economy is devastating for the bond market. Here are the indicators that we believe foretell the bond market collapse and the beginning of the nuclear winter:

- **Federal Reserve:** Begins tightening interest rates.
- **Employment:** Rises.
- **Housing starts and sales:** Rise.
- **Consumer confidence:** Rises.
- **Treasury yields:** Rise, and bond prices fall.
- **Federal debt:** Rises.
- **Bond fund flows:** Watch this very closely. At the first sign of a sustained decline of inflows, which threatens to turn to outflows, get out immediately.
- **The TIC figure:** If foreign investment in U.S. Treasurys declines, then watch for interest rates to rise. The perception is that the foreign investors who aren't buying U.S. Treasurys will continue *not* to buy. The U.S. Treasury must increase interest rates to attract investors. When this happens, bond funds will decline in value.
- **The economy:** Gets much stronger.

Several of these indicators going in one direction mean that something is happening to interest rates. Use them to determine which way. If rates seem to be going up, then exit your bond funds. Do not wait around, hoping for divine insight. That's what the rest of the herd is doing. Make your decision and execute.

Exiting Bond Funds

Bond funds have been a haven for small investors. When the bond market begins its collapse, it will take down small investors just as readily as the mega-fund institutions. Here's the answer for small investors without the capital ($500,000 to $1 million) to replace their bond funds with a diversified laddered portfolio of individual bonds: Buy various types of specialized bond funds. Here are a few:

Bond Unit Investment Trusts

A bond unit investment trust (UIT) is a portfolio of securities selected by the sponsor's managers. Bond UITs are either taxable or tax advantaged. The fixed income UIT may include U.S. Treasurys and other U.S. agencies. Investors receive monthly, quarterly, or semiannual income.

The tax-advantaged bond UIT features a portfolio of municipal bonds. Since they're munis, they generate monthly or semiannual tax-free income. If you don't live in the state of issue, the interest may be subject to state and local taxes.

The advantage of UITs for small investors is that they know just what securities their UIT holds. They also know the various maturity dates and the income stream it generates. Because of the static portfolio, investors do not worry about portfolio turnover, reduction of income (unless there's a default), or investors stampeding out.

Each unit investment trust contains a number of bonds to create a diversified portfolio. Minimum investment is usually from $1,000 to $5,000. Fees are high, so shop around.

Floating Rate Funds

These maintain a fixed spread to a benchmark rate. As interest rates rise, so will interest income from the floating rate funds. Again, this is a strategy for a rising interest rate environment.

Two such floating rate funds are the Fidelity Floating Rate High Income Fund (FFRHX, minimum investment $2,500) and the Oppenheimer Senior Floating Rate (XOSAX, minimum investment $1,000). There are others. Be sure that you shop their expense ratios before buying.

Floating rate funds bring credit risk into the equation. A rising interest rate environment produces fiscal pressure on the issuer to make good its commitment in a market that is moving against it. That's why the rates on floaters are often higher—to compensate investors for the additional risk they're taking.

Floating rate funds often employ collateral to secure the issuer's pledge to investors. Should the issuer default, the creditors' committee can liquidate the collateral to make themselves whole.

Floating Rate Loan Funds

A wrinkle in the floating rate securities market is with floating rate bank loans. These are usually closed-end funds. The funds invest in floating rate first-position bank loans pegged to the LIBOR rate. When interest rates rise, the interest paid by the borrowers to the funds also rises. An example is the $1.2 billion ING Senior Income Fund (XSIAX). It is 100 percent invested in floating-rate bank loans.

Some investors use floating rate loan funds as a hedge for their regular bond portfolio when interest rates move upward. Note that floating rate loan funds are not risk free. In fact, they seem to have somewhat of a schizophrenic performance history. During 2008, they lost an average of 27 percent. During 2009, they made this up by rising 41 percent.

They also have a first lien on assets should things go south for the borrowers. Nevertheless, default risk does exist. You are asking that the borrowers continue to honor the floating rate loan contract in a rising interest rate environment that is going against them.

End-Date Bond Funds

This is a bond ETF designed to expire at a specific future date. Buying short-duration end-date bond funds reduces interest rate risk. Since investors know when these funds will mature, they can play the duration game. If they believe interest rates will rise, they will buy an end-date fund that matures sooner rather than later. This allows it to maintain its value under the circumstances of rising rates better than a fund with a longer end date.

There are two types of end-date bond funds: municipal and corporate. The municipal end-date funds come from iShares. Like other ETFs, they track an index. In this case, that index is AMT-free, investment-grade, non-callable municipal bonds. This means they are not subject to the alternative minimum tax. They provide income either monthly or quarterly. Here are the iShares end-date municipal bond funds:

- iShares 2012 S&P AMT-Free Municipal Series (MUAA)
- iShares 2013 S&P AMT-Free Municipal Series (MUAB)
- iShares 2014 S&P AMT-Free Municipal Series (MUAC)
- iShares 2015 S&P AMT-Free Municipal Series (MUAD)
- iShares 2016 S&P AMT-Free Municipal Series (MUAE)
- iShares 2017 S&P AMT-Free Municipal Series (MUAF)

Guggenheim Fund seems to be among the more popular corporate end-date bond funds. They work the same way as the municipal bonds end-date funds. As the bonds mature, the manager invests the cash in 13-week Treasurys or similar cash equivalents until the entire ETF matures. At that point, the investors receive the funds. Here are the Guggenheim maturity-date corporate ETFs:

- Guggenheim BulletShares 2011 Corporate Bond ETF (NYSEArca: BSCB)
- Guggenheim BulletShares 2012 Corporate Bond ETF (NYSEArca: BSCC)
- Guggenheim BulletShares 2013 Corporate Bond ETF (NYSEArca: BSCD)
- Guggenheim BulletShares 2014 Corporate Bond ETF (NYSEArca: BSCE)
- Guggenheim BulletShares 2015 Corporate Bond ETF (NYSEArca: BSCF)
- Guggenheim BulletShares 2016 Corporate Bond ETF (NYSEArca: BSCG)
- Guggenheim BulletShares 2017 Corporate Bond ETF (NYSEArca: BSCH)

At the time this book went to press, these Guggenheim Bullet Shares were overweighted with bonds issued by financial institutions. About six months before maturity, most end-date fund managers open a new fund to replace the one maturing. That way, investors always have funds of the right maturity from which to choose.

By now, we know how to identify movements in the economy and inter-est rates. We know how to construct a bond portfolio fallout shelter that will survive the nuclear winter. We understand the impacts of inflation and defla-tion. Finally, we know how bond funds should behave when the bond mar-ket suffers its coming collapse. The next step, in Chapter 6, "Financial Triage Center," is to assess the damage to your own portfolio that the collapse will have caused. We'll cover assessment, prognosis for recovery, and action steps.

FINANCIAL TRIAGE CENTER

"The bubble has burst."

Neo heard his mentor's words through the telephone's earpiece. He turned over in bed to look at the clock. 5:30 A.M. The words slowly sank into his still-groggy mind. "Burst? The bubble has burst?"

Greedo's excited voice came through the earpiece, "That's what I said, my sleepy partner. Get up and get dressed. Get yourself over to the War Room. We have a family's future to save."

Neo threw off the covers and hit the floor at a run. This was the day they both had feared. "We're not ready," he muttered, quickly turning on the shower taps. *But who is ever ready for this?* he thought, stepping into the hard spray. It would be a long, trying day.

■ ■ ■

El Greedo and his brother-in-law/partner had indeed been planning for what they knew was the beginning of the bond bear market. They had educated themselves. They thought they understood the signposts that foretold the coming cataclysm. Indeed, they had been watching each of the eight indicators identified in Chapter 1 get worse and worse for months. El Greedo's early morning assessment came as no surprise to either man. The fact is they were more ready to take action than most investors. Here's an account of the triage they performed to save their family's financial future.

Checking the Indicators

If you know what to look for, there are a number of signs that will tell you the bond market has started its tumble. The difficulty is first in believing what you see and second in having the courage to take the necessary actions to protect your portfolio.

Day 1: War Room, 6:09 A.M.

Neo rushed into the War Room. Actually, it was really just Greedo's home office with a second desk and computer added for Neo's work. Their name for this room began as a joke over a year ago. As Neo learned more about the financial devastation a bond bear market would cause for so many millions of investors, it ceased being funny. Neo now thought of what they were doing as financial combat. There were forces trying to take away the nest egg his family needed to live on. He and Greedo would fight them for every last cent.

"What do our bond market indicators say today?" asked Neo, plunging down into the chair in front of his workstation and punching into their system.

"Here's what we got," said Greedo. "It's not pretty and getting worse."

Greedo looked over his former student's shoulder. "Look at the unemployment trend. See it falling? Tomorrow's the first Friday of the month. Unemployment numbers are due out at 8:30 A.M. East Coast time. My people say it'll be the lowest number yet."

Neo traced the downward-sloping graph. "That would make it seven consecutive months of rising employment—"

"Then there are housing starts and sales. They're rising a little. That doesn't look so bad."

"Yeah, but you can't trust that number," said Neo. "It has a lot of things going on—foreclosure sales, short sales, building permits that were pulled but not used because the financing fell out of bed. Still, as housing rises, we're going to see interest rates start climbing. Bad news for our bond portfolio."

"Glad you're with me, pal." The pressure must be getting to salty old Greedo. "Pull up the results of the U.S. Treasury holdings."

Neo's keyboard clattered away. Up popped the TIC figure on the U.S. Treasury's web site. "Oh, boy. Not good. China didn't buy any U.S. Treasurys. In fact, they're sellers. China cut their holdings by 2.5 percent."

"That's what caught my attention," said Greedo. "When I saw that an hour ago, I knew we needed to act today. The Chinese stopped increasing their purchases six months ago and gradually cut back—"

Neo interrupted, "Yes, and today's auction went badly. China may have even been a net seller. We won't know for sure until we get the next TIC figure in 60 days. Now the U.S. Treasury has to raise the rates it offers to give other investors like Japan and the UK an incentive to take up the slack from China. That's a huge gap to fill."

"Investors think that China is down on U.S. Treasurys and they'll probably continue cutting their allocation to our debt." Greedo wiped a hand through his hair. "More upward pressure on interest rates. What's going on with the City of San Alita? Any news?"

Neo's fingers flew across the keyboard. "San Alita, our distressed neighbor to the south." He read the screen. "Oh geez. I was afraid of that. They failed to make the interest payment on that $100 million in municipal bonds they issued. This press report says they may declare bankruptcy and seek Chapter 9 protection as early as Monday."

"If San Alita goes under, that'll be the first big American city to fail—population 8 million. Others will follow right on their heels. Our munis will take the biggest hit ever." Greedo stood up and looked at his partner.

"The bond bubble has truly burst," said Neo.

"'Fraid so. Today's the day we stop the bleeding before it's too late. Pull up the portfolio and let's figure out where to start."

■ ■ ■

The family's fixed income portfolio consists of just three categories: corporate bonds, municipal bonds, and bond funds. Take a look at the positions they've built in Table 6.1.

Table 6.1 Portfolio Appraisals with Yield to Worst—All Portfolios
Beginning Portfolio Before Triage

Settlement Date	Face Value	Security	Coupon	Maturity	Purchase Price	Total Cost	% of Assets	Yield to Maturity	Yield to Worst	Modified Duration
Corporate Bonds										
01/15/04	$100,000	Honest Mortgage, Inc.	7.000%	08/15/13	91.000	$91,000	1%	8.383%	7.842%	6.515
08/29/10	160,000	Drilling For You, Inc.	6.157%	02/15/15	96.000	153,600	2%	7.221%	7.221%	3.809
06/15/09	140,000	Operating Companies, Inc.	5.000%	01/15/16	96.000	134,400	2%	5.737%	5.737%	5.394
08/29/08	160,000	Oil Slick International	8.750%	01/25/16	95.000	152,000	2%	9.709%	9.709%	5.249
11/15/08	185,000	Big Bank, Inc.	5.500%	06/15/16	95.000	175,750	2%	6.340%	6.340%	5.928
09/20/09	140,000	Laptop Computers Internat'l	7.780%	06/04/17	98.000	137,200	2%	8.131%	8.131%	5.559
09/20/09	140,000	Credit Cards R Us	6.250%	07/15/17	99.000	138,600	2%	6.413%	6.413%	6.032
10/01/07	190,000	Pharma Drug Holdings, Inc.	6.000%	09/13/17	91.000	172,900	2%	7.287%	6.880%	7.217
04/03/09	100,000	BioTech Logic, Inc.	5.750%	07/15/18	99.000	99,000	1%	5.890%	5.890%	7.015
09/12/09	85,000	American Telecom	4.750%	02/15/19	98.000	83,300	1%	5.018%	5.018%	7.471
12/15/09	190,000	Online Brokerage Inc.	7.000%	03/01/19	93.000	176,700	2%	8.090%	8.090%	6.441
09/01/10	140,000	Sleep EZ Matress Co.	6.950%	04/01/19	125.799	176,119	2%	3.451%	3.451%	6.585
02/03/00	100,000	Steak House Inc.	7.000%	12/15/19	88.000	88,000	1%	8.236%	8.236%	9.919
08/01/06	100,000	Tanning Factory, Int'l	10.250%	03/10/20	100.125	100,125	1%	10.230%	10.230%	6.981
06/15/07	150,000	4 Corners Community Bank	8.750%	04/15/20	95.500	143,250	2%	9.357%	9.357%	7.376
09/25/10	170,000	Government Motors Acceptance Corpl	4.000%	07/15/20	100.000	170,000	2%	3.999%	3.999%	7.985

04/27/10	98,000	Electric Car USA	8.000%	07/25/20	85.000	83,300	1%	10.412%	10.412%	6.400
08/29/10	160,000	Government Motors, Inc.	3.000%	08/20/20	102.000	163,200	2%	2.769%	2.769%	8.585
03/03/09	200,000	Gold Mining, Inc.	9.000%	02/15/22	98.000	196,000	2%	9.267%	9.267%	7.464
06/15/04	185,000	Lock N Load Arms Corp.	8.650%	01/15/27	98.750	182,688	2%	8.777%	8.777%	9.439
07/25/09	240,000	Big Fat Chunky Cookie, Inc.	6.875%	05/25/30	78.000	187,200	2%	9.278%	9.278%	9.553
Subtotal Corp	$3,133,000					$3,004,331	35%			
Municipal Bonds										
08/20/10	$350,000	San Francisco Airport Commn	5.000%	01/01/12	98.000	$343,000	4%	6.551%	6.551%	1.285
06/05/09	275,000	Alita, CA	3.375%	06/15/14	85.250	234,438	3%	6.896%	6.896%	4.393
04/12/08	250,000	Phoenix, AZ GO bond	4.750%	07/01/16	98.760	246,900	3%	4.934%	4.934%	6.636
06/05/09	140,000	Bell, CA	4.000%	08/01/17	91.998	128,797	1%	5.216%	5.216%	6.704
11/17/08	100,000	Millersville, CA Redev Agy	4.000%	08/01/17	88.000	88,000	1%	5.772%	5.772%	7.036
07/12/09	210,000	Lower Colo Riv Auth. TEX	4.500%	05/15/18	102.010	214,221	2%	4.225%	3.363%	7.206
10/14/08	200,000	Hays TEX Cons indpt. Sch. Dist	4.000%	08/15/18	99.240	198,480	2%	4.094%	4.094%	8.004
04/30/07	125,000	Evanston IL	4.000%	01/01/19	99.250	124,063	1%	4.081%	4.081%	9.119
06/09/10	380,000	Shelby Cnty Tenn	4.750%	03/01/19	101.000	383,800	4%	4.609%	3.341%	7.003
08/26/10	350,000	Smith World Congress Cntr	5.500%	07/01/20	100.000	350,000	4%	5.499%	5.490%	7.465

(continued)

Table 6.1 (Continued)

Settlement Date	Face Value	Security	Coupon	Maturity	Purchase Price	Total Cost	% of Assets	Yield to Maturity	Yield to Worst	Modified Duration
11/07/07	275,000	Buckyeye Ohio Tobacco Settlement	5.130%	06/01/24	99.600	273,900	3%	5.166%	5.166%	10.817
08/31/10	100,000	Las Vegas Monorail	5.625%	01/01/32	87.250	87,250	1%	6.761%	6.761%	11.529
06/01/10	170,000	Mobile Cnty Ala	4.500%	06/01/34	98.818	167,991	2%	4.582%	4.582%	14.522
Subtotal Muni	$2,925,000					$2,840,839	33%			
Subtotal bond portfolio only						$5,845,170	67%			
Average Weighted Yields for bond portfolio only								6.285%	6.149%	
Average Weighted Duration for bond portfolio only										7.128
Bond Funds										
08/26/10	N/A	Oppenheimer PA Municipal Class C	N/A	N/A	8.000	$1,430,000	16%	N/A	N/A	N/A
08/26/09	N/A	Rochester Municipals Class C	N/A	N/A	13.100	1,410,765	16%	N/A	N/A	N/A
Subtotal Bond Funds	N/A					$2,840,765	33%			
Total Portfolio						$8,685,935	100%			

Financial Triage

America learned how to triage wounded and dying patients first in Viet Nam, then later in Iraq and Afghanistan. When you have an entire battlefield full of wounded with limited resources to treat them, medical personnel must make decisions on whom to save. They treat those in the most danger first; do what they can to stabilize them; then quickly move on to the next.

What Greedo and Neo are doing is treating the most severely injured positions first. They're working on each position in their bond portfolio. Their job is to assess which positions are in the most danger and surgically remove them.

Day 1: War Room, 7:31 A.M.

Neo looked over the Portfolio Appraisal Report he printed from the automated e-workbook. "We have corporates, munis, and bond funds. About $8.7 million worth of positions—"

"That could go to hell in a hand-basket in the next few months if we don't take action now." Greedo snatched the report from Neo. "Used to be $9 million right after I sold Greedo'z Partz and before I began trading."

"Yeah, but look how far you've recovered," said Neo.

"I lost a million of it from overconcentrating on the financials back in 2009 and 2010. I got killed."

"Not killed, my wife's brother. You recovered almost three-quarters of your loss. You were on your way to getting back the rest. Then, this happens. You're smarter than before. And, you're acting before the average investor even knows what danger he's in. Besides, you have one new, very potent weapon in your arsenal."

Greedo looked across the desk. "Yeah? What's that?"

"Me. Let's get moving. What's first?"

■ ■ ■

Good question. We're not sure what will kick off the bond bear market. No one is. When it happens, financial triage requires selling the positions that will drop the fastest and replacing them with securities that will sustain their value during the decline and the nuclear winter that follows.

Everyone has different positions in their portfolios. Greedo's, however, is typical of an average individual investor. His bond funds are a problem he needs to fix immediately or they'll drag him down. Here's what he did to stanch the bleeding.

Day 1: War Room, 8:14 A.M.

Greedo held his face in his hands for just a moment, thinking. "Okay. First, we look at the bond funds."

"Really?"

"Yeah. We're probably behind the institutions' exit, but I'll bet we're ahead of the average Joe who owns them. It's early in the game. What's the outflow of both funds?"

Neo pulled up his online funds flow news service. "I don't see any panic in either one, El."

"Okay, let's hold off on making a decision about them. They're both muni bond funds—one in Pennsylvania munis, the other in New York munis. But maybe we have some time—"

"And the value is stable so far," said Neo. "Johnny-six-pack investor is still throwing money into these funds. Excess demand is keeping up the unit price."

Greedo was thinking ten steps ahead. "Yeah, but it takes just one big institution to move the unit price versus a thousand Johnny-six-packs as you so condescendingly characterize them. I remind you, my all-too-glib brother-in-law, I am Johnny-six-pack and proud of it.

"Moving on," continued Greedo, "With the default of San Alita, I see muni values tanking. There will be a general fear in the market. It will taint all munis. Then, if San Alita files for Chapter 9 bankruptcy, we may see a slew of other cities doing the same thing."

"Why?" asked Neo. "Just because one city filed, you expect others will follow?"

Greedo glanced out the window and watched his neighbor walking by with his Labrador retriever at the end of a leash. *Poor sap*, he thought, *doesn't know what is about to happen to his investment income. He's just like me before I took matters into my own hands.*

He said to Neo, "Sure, there will be other cities that file for bankruptcy protection. Especially if bankruptcy gets San Alita out from under their $2.8 billion unfunded pension liability. What city manager wouldn't want that?"

"Got it," said Neo. "Even so, our muni funds were stable as of yesterday's close. We should be okay for a while."

Day 2: War Room, 5:30 A.M.

Greedo walked into the War Room. He was startled to see Neo already there, working at his computer. The guy already had a cup of coffee in front of him. It was half empty, he noticed.

"Just to check how much more time we have left," said Greedo, "what's going on with those bond funds?"

Neo punched up yesterday's closing price for both funds. *"Oh, my gosh*, El, they both dived—3 percent in just one day."

"WHAT?"

El Greedo kicked the carpet in frustration. "What's that? A $50,000 loss in one day for both bond funds combined?"

"More like $84,000. We waited too long. Should have kept to our game plan," said Neo.

"I was the one," moaned Greedo. "I waited too long. It was my decision."

Neo told him, "No, it wasn't just you. I'm to blame as much as you. But blame doesn't get us anywhere, does it."

Greedo hated selling a losing position. It was like admitting defeat forever with no way to make it back. "Okay. We're closing out the Rochester Municipal fund and the Oppenheimer Pennsylvania fund in their entirety. That's $2.8 million we're moving to cash. Do it. Remember that from now on we sell into an up market and buy into one that's falling."

The computer keys clattered away as Neo executed the order. "The money will be available for redeployment on Tuesday. I'm working on where to put it. Next?"

■ ■ ■

Greedo just made another mistake. He sold his entire bond fund position all at once with no strategic place to immediately invest the proceeds. He panicked. We said in Chapter 5 that investors should sell a *part* of their bond funds no larger than they can immediately reinvest in individual bonds with final maturities. Once you've deployed that money, then sell off another part and reinvest that. Keep chipping away like this until you've exhausted the bond funds.

While a loss of $84,000 appears daunting, it's less than 1 percent of the entire portfolio. Failing to have a strategic home for the money freed from the bond funds is a costly mistake. It gets more costly the longer the two investors take to find the optimum home for this $2.8 million.

ACTION STEP: PLAN YOUR WORK/WORK YOUR PLAN

When you decide on a strategy, do not second-guess yourself. Execute—even if it means you're selling a profitable position that is still rising or a losing position that you think might come back. Markets can turn in a day or less. Worst-case, you don't participate in some upside. Best-case, trade a small loss for what could be a much larger loss. Do not go down with a sinking ship just for your ego's sake.

There's another point. The partners lost that $84,000 unnecessarily. But they learned a lesson that will later save them 10 times that amount. We'll show you why these two bond funds were such a dumb buy in the Bond Fund Triage section below.

Day 2: War Room, 7:46 A.M.

Neo hung up the phone. "That was our broker at Morgan. I called to ask him to look on his Bloomberg machine and tell me what Treasury yields were doing."

"And?"

"And, he says they're up 20 basis points today."

Greedo thought for a moment. "Okay, the Federal Reserve is getting ready to raise interest rates. That's going to cause more of a selloff in the bond market."

"Agreed," said Neo. "*Marilyn Cohen's Bond Smart Investor* just had an article about corporate bond spreads widening. They email it to me soon as it's published. They say historically that's a sure sign rates are going to rise. Then, of course, there's the Conference Board's Consumer Confidence Index—it's rising."

Greedo muttered an expletive under his breath. He now knew their key indicators pointed in a definite downward direction for the bond market.

Bond Fund Triage

This is the sector where so many investors get their lunch eaten. You think a bond fund has a lot of different positions and that diversification is what makes them safe. So investors back the trucks into the loading dock and start piling those bond funds into their portfolios. We can almost hear the backup *beep-beep*ing as they do it. The brokers are only too happy to serve as enablers.

Diversification isn't a bad strategy to preserve capital. The problem comes when investors forget to look closely at the actual bond positions their fund holds. Often they're unduly concentrated in risky bonds that give an immediate uptick in yield. This attracts more investors and the fund gets richer. This is what happened to El Greedo. Take a look at his two bond funds in Table 6.2.

Now look at the bond fund by region report from the accompanying e-workbook shown in Figure 6.1.

Neo looked up from his e-workbook reports. "You know, El, that $84,000 we lost in those two bond funds yesterday?"

Greedo scowled, "Let's just move on, shall we?"

"We will, but not until we both learn the real lesson here, painful as it is. It cost us $84,000. Let's at least learn not to test the pool's depth by jumping in with both feet."

That caught Greedo's attention. He looked from his own computer screen to the newly minted bond analyst sitting across from him.

Neo said, "There are a couple of things, actually. First is that those two bond funds are completely concentrated in just two states—Pennsylvania and New York. They're not even at opposite ends of the country. We thought we were diversified. The fact was we incurred geographic risk. Next, both had huge fees—"

"Yeah, they did. But what about the Oppenheimer fund?"

"Both are Oppenheimer funds. The Rochester fund just leaves out the Oppenheimer name. You did a great job with both for a while, my yield-hungry relative. You bought after the crash in 2008 and you rode it up through 2010." Neo looked at Greedo's puzzled expression. "You're wondering what happened. I know what happened. We forgot to study the credit quality of the actual bonds the funds held. Turns out the Oppenheimer PA fund was heavily invested in poor-credit-quality bonds. When the market was rising these bonds rose right along with it. That's why our yield was up. But, soon as the market began falling, the credit-challenged bonds led the descent. The Oppenheimer PA fund got whacked."

Greedo hung his head. "I trusted Oppi to stick to its prospectus. I never once looked at the bonds it held."

Table 6.2 Portfolio Appraisal with Yield to Worst—All Portfolios
Beginning Portfolio Before Triage—Bond Funds

Settlement Date	Face Value	Security	Coupon	Maturity	Purchase Price	Total Cost	% of Assets	Yield to Maturity	Yield to Worst	Modified Duration
Bond Funds										
08/26/10	N/A	Oppenheimer PA Municipal Class C	N/A	N/A	8.000	$1,430,000	16%	N/A	N/A	N/A
08/26/09	N/A	Rochester Municipals Class C	N/A	N/A	13.100	1,410,765	16%	N/A	N/A	N/A
Subtotal Bond Funds	N/A					$2,840,765	33%			

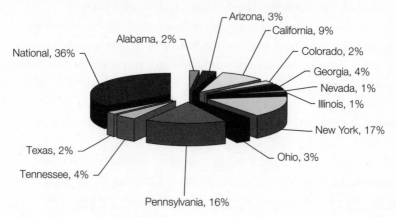

Asset Allocation (Region): All Portfolios

Figure 6.1   Bond Fund by Region

"Oh, it stuck to the prospectus all right. But the Rochester prospectus also said it could invest in tobacco-settlement bonds, hospital bonds, and revenue bonds. These are the riskiest of all bonds. When the market falls out of bed, these are the first to go and they'll keep on going down."

Greedo said, "We didn't stand a chance."

"But that's the last time we're making such a mistake. Now, we have $2.8 million in cash that needs a temporary home. We can't leave it hanging out there without any earnings even for one day. Where do you want it to go?"

Greedo spun around in his chair so he was facing his suddenly-so-smart relative. "*Geez,* I hadn't thought of that. It's gotta be insulated from any more loss. At least until we can intelligently place it. Where do you think?"

"Glad you asked," said Neo. "This is financial triage. We stopped the bleeding by selling those two funds. But we need a short-term home. The Vanguard National Money Market Fund is my choice. It's safe. Yield sucks, but the money won't be there for very long. And it's liquid for when we make our decision to redeploy that money. You okay with that?"

"Do it. While you're doing that, I'll get out the muni bond portfolio report. Let's see what holdings are most vulnerable there."

Municipal Bond Triage

Greedo just made a financial triage decision. He suspects that the municipal bond prices are vulnerable. Right now he's running the e-workbook report that isolates just the munis. With that information, he has positioned himself to determine which municipal bonds to sell and which to keep.

The first municipal bonds to get rid of are those that are abscessing, blistering, and fulminating. **Look for bonds whose issuers are making negative headlines.** News reports on city council meetings turned to riot because of the financially inane things the Council did are good examples of negative headlines. Watch for other sources of negative publicity, such as economic reports that show residential census declining in municipalities whose bonds you own. Such headline risk drags down bond prices.

Next, find out the extent of your **issuers' unfunded liabilities,** such as pensions and public employee health benefits. In some cases, these are greater than the city's entire annual revenue. For such municipalities, there is no way out of that hole. Their bonds will die a painful death.

Overspending is another foreshadowing of municipal bond problems. Check to see how the property tax revenue is doing for your issuer compared to its budget. If you see expenses exceeding revenue with the hope that floating another bond issue will fill the gap, you know there is a problem. This is called *kicking the can down the road.* The elected incumbents are just papering over a problem until the next election. They have ignored the tough decisions they were elected to make in favor of bettering their chances for reelection.

Sales tax revenues are another sign of problems. Check the issuer's sales tax rate. Many states, counties, and cities have already set sales taxes at the maximum. Residents and companies that decide they cannot afford to live there will leave. When that happens, there is no room to raise revenue.

Nonessential Service Bonds

Investors will argue about what exactly constitutes a nonessential service. After all, if the bonds weren't essential in the first place, why would the voters have approved them? The general rule is that nonessential service bonds are for truly discretionary assets. They often rely on the revenue produced by the asset the bonds bought to service the debt.

The bond market historically discounts the value of nonessential service bonds during difficult economic times. The thinking is that a nonessential service revenue bond is far more likely to default than bonds issued for things that residents absolutely, positively cannot live without—such as water and sewer services.

New sports arenas and stadiums are certainly not essential to a municipality's survival. Yes, they may provide a badly needed injection of revenue dollars to the business community. However, in a down economy, or even if the home team is just languishing in last place, fans will not visit the ballpark to take in the game. Revenue counted on to service the bond interest and principal payments will fall short of what is required. The bonds may well default.

The City of Las Vegas's monorail system is a good example of a bad $650 million nonessential service bond. During the economic decline of 2008–2009 visitors to Las Vegas dropped to a fraction of the average. Very few people paid to use the monorail. The City built it in the wrong place. Its revenue and expense forecasts were *way* off the mark. The bond issue defaulted. Guess who owns them—Greedo. He's going to have a fit a bit later in this chapter when he finds out.

Overspending Municipalities

We anticipate the bond market's nuclear winter to reflect the exact opposite of the overall U.S. economy. The economy is heating up. The U.S. dollar is falling; interest rates are rising—and the bond market is tanking. Cities issue bonds to pay for all sorts of things that made sense at the time: new civic centers, new fire stations, new police stations, and new courthouses, among many other purposes. However, budgetary purse strings can pull very tight, very quickly.

The city suddenly finds that it has *way* overspent. Its revenues are now insufficient to cover its obligations. The Las Vegas monorail default left bond investors holding an empty bag.

Look for overspending issuers in the munis you hold. When you find them, get out of the bonds. Table 6.3 is a snapshot of the municipal bond portfolio component Greedo and Neo are talking about.

Neo said to Greedo, "So I'm going over the municipal bond section of the Portfolio Appraisal Report from the e-workbook. You know you still have those City of Bell, CA, bonds? That's $140,000 face value in headline risk right there—"

"What? I thought I got rid of those. You sure?"

"I'm sure, my overburdened partner. We talked about selling them when it first surfaced that the mayor's salary was almost $800,000 a year. You said you'd take care of it."

Table 6.3 Portfolio Appraisal with Yield to Worst—All Portfolios
Beginning Portfolio Before Triage—Municipal Bonds

Settlement Date	Face Value	Security	Coupon	Maturity	Purchase Price	Total Cost	% of Assets	Yield to Maturity	Yield to Worst	Modified Duration
Municipal Bonds										
08/20/10	$350,000	San Francisco Airport Commn	5.000%	01/01/12	98.000	$343,000	4%	6.551%	6.551%	1.285
06/05/09	275,000	Alita, CA	3.375%	06/15/14	85.250	234,438	3%	6.896%	6.896%	4.393
04/12/08	250,000	Phoenix, AZ GO bond	4.750%	07/01/16	98.760	246,900	3%	4.934%	4.934%	6.636
06/05/09	140,000	Bell, CA	4.000%	08/01/17	91.998	128,797	1%	5.216%	5.216%	6.704
11/17/08	100,000	Millersville, CA Redev Agy	4.000%	08/01/17	88.000	88,000	1%	5.772%	5.772%	7.036
07/12/09	210,000	Lower Colo Riv Auth. TEX	4.500%	05/15/18	102.010	214,221	2%	4.225%	3.363%	7.206
10/14/08	200,000	Hays TEX Cons indpt. Sch. Dist	4.000%	08/15/18	99.240	198,480	2%	4.094%	4.094%	8.004
04/30/07	125,000	Evanston IL	4.000%	01/01/19	99.250	124,063	1%	4.081%	4.081%	9.119
06/09/10	380,000	Shelby Cnty Tenn	4.750%	03/01/19	101.000	383,800	4%	4.609%	3.341%	7.003
08/26/10	350,000	Geo. Smith World Congress Cntr	5.500%	07/01/20	100.000	350,000	4%	5.499%	5.490%	7.465
11/07/07	275,000	Buckyeye Ohio Tobacco Settlement	5.130%	06/01/24	99.600	273,900	3%	5.166%	5.166%	10.817
08/31/10	100,000	Las Vegas Monorail	5.625%	01/01/32	87.250	87,250	1%	6.761%	6.761%	11.529
06/01/10	170,000	Mobile Cnty Ala	4.500%	06/01/34	98.818	167,991	2%	4.582%	4.582%	14.522
Subtotal Muni	$2,925,000					$2,840,839	33%			

Greedo scratched his chin, "I remember. Those bonds were down 10 percent then. I just couldn't take the hit. I hoped they'd come back."

Neo's keyboard clattered away. "TRACE says they're down to 66. That's a shocking haircut from where you bought them, El."

"Sell the bastards," grumbled Greedo. "What else does the Appraisal Report say?"

Neo scrolled through the Portfolio Appraisal Report on his screen. "There are two more I don't like. One is the San Francisco Airport bond."

"What about it? It's the airport. Should be safe."

Neo looked over his computer screen at his brother-in-law. "El, it's not really the airport. I looked at the Official Statement. It's actually a revenue bond for a fueling facility. Neither the city, the airport, nor the county guarantees this bond. *Nada.* And its interest coverage is just 1.0. If anything happens to disturb that revenue stream, they'll default for sure. We paid $343,000 for those bonds. We gotta sell.

"The second is the Buckeye Ohio Tobacco Settlement bonds. When interest rates start climbing, these things will turn and burn worse than they already are. Smoking is down; taxes on tobacco products are way up and climbing. I don't see how they can sustain this kind of debt service. Okay to put them on our dump list, too?"

El Greedo nodded. "How do you know all these things?"

"I'm just doing what every bond holder needs to do before the market collapses. I'm going through every single position and asking myself what could go wrong. It takes a ton of time. I've been here since 4:00 A.M. But it's something we must do right now before things get any worse."

"You are right. Pull up the Millersville California bond. This is one that's bothering me."

Neo clicked on the Current Portfolio Screen. "Got it. What's up?"

"Okay. Here's what scares me about Millersville. I asked our broker to send me their financials. What he sent was the 2006 financials. But the city filed them in 2010. What's that about? Four years late? So I began digging to find what they're hiding."

"And? What did you find?"

Greedo tossed the hardcopy portfolio reports on the desk with a slap. "What I found was a rising crime rate in Riverdale County. The property tax rolls are declining. But without current financials, who the hell knows how the bonds will fare. I say sell 'em."

Neo made a note to sell on his portfolio position listing. "Okay. We have some Las Vegas Monorail and City of Alita, CA, bonds. Let's get rid of those while we're at it."

"The Vegas monorail? "Greedo let fly a stream of expletives." I thought I sold those things. Vegas tourism in 2009 and 2010 was almost nonexistent. The monorail goes in back of the hotels it serves rather than in front of them like normal people use. Who wants to walk all the way around the back of those monster buildings for a two-minute ride?" He dropped his pencil on the desk in disgust with himself. "Sell them. Do it now."

"We might want to wait," suggested Neo. "The Vegas bonds are already in default. They're not worth much now. I say we keep 'em and hope we're made whole. That's a loss of $60,000. TRACE says the price has stabilized since they defaulted. Yes, let's keep them. What about San Alita?"

Greedo shook his head, still smarting from the Vegas monorail bonds. "San Alita has such a huge unfunded pension liability—over $2 billion. Yeah, let's dump them and put the money to better use."

"While we're at it," said Neo, "Let's get rid of the Smith World Center bonds. It's a nonessential bond, similar to a sports stadium. Okay?"

"Right. Neo, you've done some job in researching the municipal bond portfolio. I had no idea you were paying such close attention to what I was teaching you."

Neo looked at his brother-in-law and wondered just what Greedo thought he'd taught him. "If you knew so much, dear Bro, how did all this happen in the first place?"

"Balls," said Greedo. "I like a guy with balls. Gotta have 'em in this game. Just shows you how complicated this all is. I mean, if a seasoned investor such as myself sometimes gets it wrong . . . anyway, now it's my turn. I'm taking ownership of the corporate bonds."

Corporate Bond Triage

Back in 2008–2009, when America's financial system teetered on the brink of going under, some major changes occurred. The bond market landscape became distorted and with it the rules of engagement. By forcing General Motors bond holders to accept equity in a new GM when the law clearly gave them first credit position, President Obama declared financial war on investors.

We also learned that U.S. government agency debt carried huge risk. When the Obama Administration placed Freddie Mac and Fannie Mae into conservatorship and then canceled all preferred stock dividends overnight, the preferred shareholders lost billions. For more of the changes that caused bond investors to rebalance their portfolios and their strategies, please see *Bonds Now!* (John Wiley & Sons, 2009).

El Greedo did just what he was supposed to do in 2008 and 2009. He rebalanced his portfolio according to the new fixed income landscape. He got out of U.S. government agencies—too risky under the Obama Administration. He got out of all complicated holdings that depended on derivative interest rates that often had little to do with the investment in the first place. His motto became, *If I don't understand it, I don't own it.* Table 6.4 shows his corporate bond portfolio before the nuclear winter bond market collapse.

Corporate Bond Assessment

Looking over Greedo's corporate bond portfolio, it seems that he has a nicely diversified portfolio. No single position accounts for more than 2 percent of the entire portfolio. He has some financials, that's true. El Greedo has always favored financials since they provide higher yields. Still, he has consumer companies, healthcare, transportation, energy, commodities, and other sectors. What's wrong here? Plenty.

■ ■ ■

"Let's begin with an obvious position," said Greedo. "I'm not willing to take much of a chance knowing what we know right now about the economy's upward trajectory. If the yield is too far above normal for that kind of company, it means there's more risk than I'm willing to take."

Neo spotted the problem immediately. "You're talking about Oil Slick International. It has a 9.7 percent yield to maturity where its brethren only have 7.75 percent. Why?"

"They're drilling 38 wells in the Gulf. It's their biggest concentration of leases. What if one, just one, well explodes? I'm worried."

Neo said, "Yes, but we're being compensated for the risk. How about we put it on the watch list? The first sign of trouble, we get out."

"Good. Next, I don't want to own Big Bank. There's a disconnect between the CEO's compensation package and the bank's poor performance. I'm not

Table 6.4 Portfolio Appraisal with Yield to Worst—All Portfolios
Beginning Portfolio Before Triage—Corporate Bonds

Settlement Date	Face Value	Security	Coupon	Maturity	Purchase Price	Total Cost	% of Assets	Yield to Maturity	Yield to Worst	Modified Duration
Corporate Bonds										
01/15/04	$100,000	Honest Mortgage, Inc.	7.000%	08/15/13	91.000	$91,000	1%	8.383%	7.842%	6.515
08/29/10	160,000	Drilling For You, Inc.	6.157%	02/15/15	96.000	153,600	2%	7.221%	7.221%	3.809
06/15/09	140,000	Operating Companies, Inc.	5.000%	01/15/16	96.000	134,400	2%	5.737%	5.737%	5.394
08/29/08	160,000	Oil Slick International	8.750%	01/25/16	95.000	152,000	2%	9.709%	9.709%	5.249
11/15/08	185,000	Big Bank, Inc.	5.500%	06/15/16	95.000	175,750	2%	6.340%	6.340%	5.928
09/20/09	140,000	Laptop Computers Internat'l	7.780%	06/04/17	98.000	137,200	2%	8.131%	8.131%	5.559
09/20/09	140,000	Credit Cards R Us	6.250%	07/15/17	99.000	138,600	2%	6.413%	6.413%	6.032
10/01/07	190,000	Pharma Drug Holdings, Inc.	6.000%	09/13/17	91.000	172,900	2%	7.287%	6.880%	7.217
04/03/09	100,000	BioTech Logic, Inc.	5.750%	07/15/18	99.000	99,000	1%	5.890%	5.890%	7.015

Par	Issuer	Coupon	Maturity	Price	Market Value	%			
85,000	American Telecom	4.750%	09/12/09	98.000	83,300	1%	5.018%	5.018%	7.471
190,000	Online Brokerage Inc.	7.000%	12/15/09	93.000	176,700	2%	8.090%	8.090%	6.441
140,000	Sleep EZ Matress Co.	6.950%	09/01/10	125.799	176,119	2%	3.451%	3.451%	6.585
100,000	Steak House Inc.	7.000%	02/03/00	88.000	88,000	1%	8.236%	8.236%	9.919
100,000	Tanning Factory, Int'l	10.250%	08/01/06	100.125	100,125	1%	10.230%	10.230%	6.981
150,000	4 Corners Community Bank	8.750%	06/15/07	95.500	143,250	2%	9.357%	9.357%	7.376
170,000	Government Motors Acceptance Corpl	4.000%	09/25/10	100.000	170,000	2%	3.999%	3.999%	7.985
98,000	Electric Car USA	8.000%	04/27/10	85.000	83,300	1%	10.412%	10.412%	6.400
160,000	Government Motors, Inc.	3.000%	08/29/10	102.000	163,200	2%	2.769%	2.769%	8.585
200,000	Gold Mining, Inc.	9.000%	03/03/09	98.000	196,000	2%	9.267%	9.267%	7.464
185,000	Lock N Load Arms Corp.	8.650%	06/15/04	98.750	182,688	2%	8.777%	8.777%	9.439
240,000	Big Fat Chunky Cookie, Inc.	6.875%	07/25/09	78.000	187,200	2%	9.278%	9.278%	9.553
Subtotal Corp	$3,133,000				$3,004,331	35%			

going to be punished while some lackluster executives line their pockets. Dump it."

■ ■ ■

It looks like Greedo did his homework. The research anyone does to arrive at such conclusions isn't difficult. In the case of Big Bank, all Greedo had to do was get the company's Form 10-K over the Internet. He immediately saw a rise in executive salaries while revenues and profits slumped.

■ ■ ■

Neo threw in his two cents: "Let's talk about Big Fat Chunky Cookie—"

"You ever had one? They're six ounces of gooey, bittersweet chocolate with walnuts spun through. Awesome."

ACTION STEP: WATCH FOR CREDITOR BAIL-IN LEGISLATION

As of this writing global bank regulators are trying to establish a system that penalizes investors in bank bonds. Here's what they have in mind: Should a bank fail, regulators would have the authority to convert bonds held by good-faith bond investors into equity—called a *bail-in*. Apparently, the Obama Administration's illegal, forced conversion of General Motors bonds into equity worked so well, the bank regulators thought they'd float a trial balloon and maybe sneak aboard. After all, they were seeing this unfold with the debt-burdened Irish banks.

The bank regulator's logic goes that converting debt, particularly subordinated debt, to equity builds the bank's capital base and allows it to stay in business longer. This avoids government bailouts and costly rescues while giving bond investors upside potential should the troubled bank somehow survive.

If passed, this authority will be devastating for corporate bonds issued by financial institutions. The cost of capital will increase due to the added risk bond holders must now assume. **Bond investors should be careful not to overallocate to the financial industry. If creditor bail-in becomes law, beware.**

Neo shook his head in disbelief. "Maybe so, but management isn't bond friendly. They're floating a $500 million bond issue to fund acquisition of National Dairy Enterprises. Horizontal integration."

"Cookies and milk. I get it," said Greedo, smiling at the thought of the salad-plate-sized pastry beside a frosty glass of milk.

"*Hello—Earth to El*. There's no common distribution channel. The manufacturing technologies for the cookies and the milk provide no synergies. The acquisition will fail. I'm not taking the risk. We sell them."

"How about Pharma Drug Holdings?" asked Greedo, now back in the ballgame.

"I'm briefed in about their new anti-depression drug. With the bond market meltdown we think is coming there are a lot of fixed income investors who will need what Pharma Drug sells. Not only that, management is bond friendly. No leveraged acquisitions. No stock buybacks funded by bond issuance just to jerk up the stock price. Let's keep it."

■ ■ ■

Something to keep in mind when assessing your corporate bond positions is the stock price. Watch for suddenly falling stock prices in companies whose bonds you own. This often foretells the coming replacement of the CEO; unpleasant quarterly numbers; or trouble renewing bank lines. When the white knight arrives, his primary job will be to get the stock price back up to where it was before. Often, the easiest, fastest way to accomplish this is by taking actions opposed to bond holders' interests. Neo is right to worry about stock buyback and acquisitions funded by new bonds. Both dilute the available cash to service existing bond debt.

It's better to hold corporate bonds issued by companies with a history of being friendly to bond holders. Such companies typically don't have a lot of leverage on their balance sheets. The board of directors insists that CEO compensation be tied to the company's performance. They hold the line on lavish equity dividends, leaving a larger cash cushion to service bond debt.

■ ■ ■

"You're on a roll now, El. What else?" Neo's sarcasm was lost on his brother-in-law.

"Okay, let me think. Oh, I know. I put $100,000 into Tanning Factory International. Thought I'd take a chance. Besides, it's the highest yielding bond in the portfolio. But tanning salons are a luxury this downward bond market spiral will reject. It's totally discretionary spending. There's one final nail in the coffin. The federal government is implementing a special tanning salon tax. Franchise owners are trying to dump their holdings on Craig's List, for goodness sake. Tanning Factory should be a corporate bond triage sale."

Neo held up his hand to get Greedo's attention. "Agreed. Consumer discretionary goods are going to be a problem if the bond market goes way south like we think it will. How about we also cut in half our position in Steak House, Inc.?"

Greedo confirmed, "*Done-ski*. I'm uncomfortable with Government Motors, the car company, and Government Motors Acceptance Corp, their finance arm. The federal government screwed us bond holders once by forcing us to trade in our bonds for equity. If things get dicey, there's nothing stopping them from doing it again." Greedo looked at his Portfolio Appraisal report. "Combined, they account for four percent of the entire portfolio. Let's get out of them both."

Neo made some notes, then said, "I want to leave Lock-N-Load Arms Corp. for now. I see their business stabilizing. People are getting angry at their elected officials. Not shooting angry. But the cities and counties can't afford the kind of police protection they had in the past. People are going to arm themselves for protection. That means more weapons sales."

Greedo wondered just how bad things were going to get in the coming nuclear winter. *Pretty bad*, he feared.

Squeezing the Trigger

Greedo is wary of companies replacing their bond-friendly CEO with someone having a reputation for not being very friendly to bond holders. However, what do you do when the company replaces your bond friendly CEO with someone whose disposition toward bond holders is unclear? If the CEO is the only reason you'd sell the bond, you might consider waiting.

■ ■ ■

"I'm looking at BioTech Logic," said Neo. "Their new CEO is an enigma."

Greedo replied, "I can't find out a thing about him, either. His predecessor delevered the company, funded acquisitions through their cash war chest, and didn't raise the stock dividend. He was an all-around great guy to us bond holders. This is a solid company. Let's give the new guy six months. If he screws us by doing something decidedly unfriendly to us bond holders, then I'll pull the trigger. Besides, it's only one percent of the portfolio."

■ ■ ■

Table 6.5 Portfolio Appraisal with Yield to Worst — Triage All Portfolios

Settlement Date	Security	Face Value	Coupon	Maturity	Purchase Price	Total Cost	% of Assets	Yield to Maturity	Yield to Worst	Modified Duration
Corporate Bonds										
01/15/04	Honest Mortgage, Inc.	$100,000	7.000%	08/15/13	91.000	$91,000	1%	8.383%	7.842%	6.515
08/29/10	Drilling For You, Inc.	160,000	6.157%	02/15/15	96.000	153,600	2%	7.221%	7.221%	3.809
06/15/09	Operating Companies, Inc.	140,000	5.000%	01/15/16	96.000	134,400	2%	5.737%	5.737%	5.394
08/29/08	Oil Slick International	160,000	8.750%	01/25/16	95.000	152,000	2%	9.709%	9.709%	5.249
09/20/09	Laptop Computers Internat'l	140,000	7.780%	06/04/17	98.000	137,200	2%	8.131%	8.131%	5.559
09/20/09	Credit Cards R Us	140,000	6.250%	07/15/17	99.000	138,600	2%	6.413%	6.413%	6.032
10/01/07	Pharma Drug Holdings, Inc.	190,000	6.000%	09/13/17	91.000	172,900	2%	7.287%	6.880%	7.217
04/03/09	BioTech Logic, Inc.	100,000	5.750%	07/15/18	99.000	99,000	1%	5.890%	5.890%	7.015
09/12/09	American Telecom	85,000	4.750%	02/15/19	98.000	83,300	1%	5.018%	5.018%	7.471
12/15/09	Online Brokerage Inc.	190,000	7.000%	03/01/19	93.000	176,700	2%	8.090%	8.090%	6.441
09/01/10	Sleep EZ Matress Co.	140,000	6.950%	04/01/19	125.799	176,119	2%	3.451%	3.451%	6.585
02/03/00	Steak House Inc.	50,000	7.000%	12/15/19	88.000	44,000	1%	8.236%	8.236%	9.919
08/01/06	Tanning Factory, Int'l	100,000	10.250%	03/10/20	100.125	100,125	1%	10.230%	10.230%	6.981
06/15/07	4 Corners Community Bank	150,000	8.750%	04/15/20	95.500	143,250	2%	9.357%	9.357%	7.376
04/27/10	Electric Car USA	98,000	8.000%	07/25/20	85.000	83,300	1%	10.412%	10.412%	6.400

(Continued)

93

Table 6.5 (Continued)

Settlement Date	Face Value	Security	Coupon	Maturity	Purchase Price	Total Cost	% of Assets	Yield to Maturity	Yield to Worst	Modified Duration
03/03/09	200,000	Gold Mining, Inc.	9.000%	02/15/22	98.000	196,000	2%	9.267%	9.267%	7.464
06/15/04	185,000	Lock N Load Arms Corp.	8.650%	01/15/27	98.750	182,688	2%	8.777%	8.777%	9.439
Subtotal Corp	$2,328,000					$2,264,181	26%			
Municipal Bonds										
04/12/08	$250,000	Phoenix, AZ GO bond	4.750%	07/01/16	98.760	$246,900	3%	4.934%	4.934%	6.636
07/12/09	210,000	Lower Colo Riv Auth. TEX	4.500%	05/15/18	102.010	214,221	2%	4.225%	3.363%	7.206
10/14/08	200,000	Hays TEX Cons indpt. Sch. Dist	4.000%	08/15/18	99.240	198,480	2%	4.094%	4.094%	8.004
04/30/07	125,000	Evanston IL	4.000%	01/01/19	99.250	124,063	1%	4.081%	4.081%	9.119
06/09/10	380,000	Shelby Cnty Tenn	4.750%	03/01/19	101.000	383,800	4%	4.609%	3.341%	7.003
08/31/10	100,000	Las Vegas Monorail	5.625%	01/01/32	87.250	87,250	1%	6.761%	6.761%	11.529
06/01/10	170,000	Mobile Cnty Ala	4.500%	06/01/34	98.818	167,991	2%	4.582%	4.582%	14.522
Subtotal Muni	$1,435,000					$1,422,704	16%			
Subtotal bond portfolio only						$3,686,885	42%			

Average Weighted Yields for bond portfolio only							6.511%	6.297%	
Average Weighted Duration for bond portfolio only									7.353
Other Securities									
11/06/10	N/A	All States Funds	N/A	$1.00	$1,666,600	19%	N/A	N/A	N/A
11/06/10	N/A	Federal Financial Funds	N/A	$1.00	1,666,000	19%	N/A	N/A	N/A
11/06/10	N/A	Fifty States Funds	N/A	$1.00	1,666,600	19%	N/A	N/A	N/A
Subtotal Other Securities	N/A		N/A		$4,999,200	58%			
Total Portfolio					$8,686,085	100%			

ACTION STEP: THE POINT ABOUT FINANCIAL TRIAGE

The point is simple: Stabilize the patient. Stop the bleeding. Get out of the most vulnerable positions—now. Don't wait. Put the money into very safe, liquid instruments until you can redeploy it to strategic positions that accomplish your goals.

The two traded their way out of almost $5 million in problem positions. They spread the money around three national money market funds. At least it is earning something until they can redeploy it.

Greedo isn't out of the woods yet. Chapter 7 shows how the positions he's left with now account for way too large a percentage of the portfolio. Worse still, they're overexposed to relatively small rises in interest rates. We'll demonstrate how to move out of emergency triage, into a solid portfolio structure designed to sustain you through the nuclear winter.

REBALANCING INTO THE NUCLEAR WINTER

There's a transition between the positions most investors have in the triage stage and in the nuclear winter stage. Triage tends to be emergency medicine for your portfolio. Investors aren't worried about long-term strategies so much as they are stopping the value of their holdings from plummeting.

We saw that panic in Greedo's dumping of the $2.8 million in bond funds. He was understandably upset over his unnecessary $84,000 loss because he waited another day after he and Neo had already made the decision to exit the bond funds. Nevertheless, with the cash from the bond funds along with the corporates and munis sold, they now have a combined total of $5 million to deploy in a rebalanced portfolio. This represents about 58 percent of their holdings sitting on the sidelines until they can work out a plan for surviving the nuclear winter.

Greedo's situation isn't uncommon for individual investors. When faced with an expectation the market is moving against them for a sustained period, many react the same way.

This chapter shows how to plan ahead to avoid panic selling like Greedo. If done correctly, you'll already know where to put cash generated from the triage stage. It then becomes a smoother transition into a portfolio designed to weather the nuclear winter.

Nuclear Winter Investment Strategy

Greedo's $5 million in cash isn't earning much sitting in those three money market accounts. However, at least he and Neo are comfortable that they're not losing money every minute. Here's how the portfolio stands after triage:

Cash:	$5.0 million
Corporates:	$2.3 million
Munis:	$1.4 million
Total:	$8.7 million

The goal of rebalancing the portfolio to withstand a sustained nuclear winter is an almost-even allocation between categories. The illustration in Figure 7.1 shows a typical even split.

The 25 percent allocation to cash or equivalents doesn't yield much but is safe and liquid. The 25 percent allocation to securities specifically designed

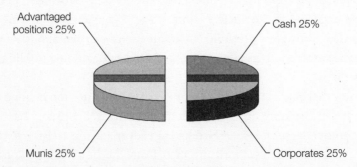

Figure 7.1   Nuclear Winter Target Allocation

to deal with a sustained down market are the LEAPS, end-date bonds, and the other types of securities discussed later in this chapter.

Investing in Cash

We said earlier that investors should keep a substantial amount of cash on hand during the nuclear winter to take advantage of the opportunities that inevitably occur. Keep in mind, that money won't be earning much of anything in the super-safe, liquid investment vehicles we'll recommend. However, that small opportunity loss balances out against the oversized gain from its future deployment. Here's how our two investment *wunderkinds* puzzle this one out:

Day 5: War Room, 8:30 A.M.

Greedo couldn't believe his ears. He wondered if his partner was suddenly gun shy. "You're telling me that you want to keep almost $2.2 million out of the bond market. For real? Or are you just trying to give me a heart attack?"

Neo held his ground. It was something he'd finally learned to do with the strong-willed brother of his wife. "Yep. We keep $2,175,000 in U.S. Treasury bills—spread out between six-month maturities and twelve-month maturities.

Greedo said, "I don't get it. That money can work harder for us by putting it in corporates or munis or LEAPS—anything but Treasurys."

"Let's not make the same mistake as other investors," advised Neo. "They always go for the immediate increase in yield."

Greedo wasn't happy. He wore the badge of the Yield Hog proudly. "Do you know how much it will cost us in below-market yield?"

"It will cost us $65,250 if we keep the entire $2,175,000 on the bench for a whole year, assuming the T-bills return on average three percent less than our other short-term investments."

Uncharacteristically, Greedo thought for a moment before speaking. "*Hmmm.* So 65 grand is the price we pay for the liquidity we need to take advantage of these opportunities you think will come our way. So, what are they?"

Neo reluctantly set down his whole-wheat bagel. "Don't know yet," he said matter-of-factly. "But they'll come. Always do. Only most investors won't have the cash to invest in them. We'll have dry powder to take to the fight for exceptional yield. Extraordinary yield."

"Got it," said Greedo. "Why settle for a single on the first pitch when you can run the count full, then jump on a home run?

■ ■ ■

Greedo understood that argument. Like Neo, we don't know what extraordinary opportunities the nuclear winter will bring to those having the willpower to keep their powder dry. Historically, sustained down markets have fostered these types of opportunities:

- Bargains in the high-yield market.
- Emerging debt opportunities.
- Investment-grade corporates with more attractive yields.
- Great municipal bond credits at bargain-basement prices.

Beefing Up Corporate Bond Holdings

Even after the spate of selling the two did during triage, they still entered the nuclear winter with $2.3 million in the corporate bond portfolio. The approximate target allocation for corporate bonds during a sustained market downturn is 25 percent.

Blue-Chip Bonds, Laddered Maturities

Put a significant percentage of your corporate bond allocation into the highest quality bonds you can get. The logic is that no matter how bad things may get during the nuclear winter, these large, stable companies are more likely to ride out the storm than their competitors of a lesser credit quality.

You already know the names. All are Fortune 500 companies. They have solid balance sheets, good management, and an abundance of cash. Their footprint is global and they are the leaders in each of their market segments. These are names such as:

- Johnson & Johnson
- Federal Express
- IBM

- Microsoft
- Disney
- McDonald's
- Exxon Mobil

Additionally, we want you to be careful with the maturities you select. These corporates should mature approximately equally over the next four years. This does two things. First, a short-term laddered maturity structure reduces the suffering from holding bonds that fall in value over the nuclear winter as interest rates rise. When they mature, you can take the money and invest it in bonds with higher yields.

Second, because you have a short ladder—just four years—the duration of the corporate portfolio is low. This reduces the negative impact of rising interest rates more than if you had longer maturities. Additionally, the nuclear winter won't last forever. Structure the portfolio to have available funds to invest as the green shoots of the bond market recovery begin to appear.

Day 10: Global Burgers Restaurant, 12:37 P.M.

"I never eat junk food like this, El. What's up?"

Greedo hefted his double-double burger and tore into another bite. He looked around at the restaurant packed with children and their parents. "I just wanted you to see my logic in real time."

Neo picked at his chilled salad in a box. "We have bonds to trade, my hungry relative. If you were hungry, I could have sent out for sandwiches. Triage is over. The bleeding is stopped. We urgently need to redeploy $5 million in idle cash."

Greedo held up a perfect French fry for inspection. "Wouldn't have been the same. Look here. It's golden, crispy. Did you know Global's signature is the very fry I'm holding here between my fingas? They first blanch them, then cook them once more but not until the customer places the order." Greedo leaned forward for confidentiality. He spoke around the French fry as he chewed. "Economy's on fire. Our bond indicators say rates are rising. Even though unemployment has shrunk, people haven't forgotten what being jobless feels like. They're valuing their dollars more. Expensive, fancy restaurants are out. I don't want to own any high-end eateries like the Steak House bonds we dumped. I'm putting that money plus some of the $5 mil you're so worried about into a major position in Global Burgers. It's not the lowest end of the restaurant food chain. But it provides high value for the money."

"When?"

"Now. Get out the laptop and let's make the trade."

Neo put down his plastic fork and opened the lid of his laptop. "What does TRACE say GBI's 4 percent of 9/3/15 trade at?" he asked Greedo.

"I checked before we left. It's bouncing around 107.25 and 106.98."

"I'm putting in a bid at 106.95 with Interactive Brokers Online," said Neo. "Wait . . . offer came back at 107 even."

"Lift the offer," ordered Greedo and took another bite of his double-double.

"Lift the offer?" questioned Neo. "What's 'lift the offer' mean?"

Greedo struggled to swallow his mouthful of burger. "*Putz*—it's professional bondspeak. Means that you should *take* the offer."

■ ■ ■

They now own 300 bonds of a stable, blue-chip company poised to survive the bond market nuclear winter. They chose this company because its target market tracks the economy that has already run up and is now moving along at the top.

This is the bond market nuclear winter strategy: Buy stable companies. Be sure they have plenty of discretionary cash. Invest in companies whose customers are right in line with the robust economy. Finally, ratchet down duration by limiting maturities to no more than four years. That way, as interest rates rise, the portfolio won't be stung too badly.

Take a look at the corporate bond portfolio in Table 7.1 that Greedo and Neo rebalanced for the nuclear winter. The names of the companies populating this nuclear winter corporate bond portfolio are fictional and unimportant. Instead, focus on the reasons Greedo put them in the portfolio.

Day 13: War Room, 2:14 P.M.

"That pretty much does it," said Neo. He stood up from his computer and stretched.

Greedo moved away from his computer as well. "I'm done, too. I never had to rebalance an entire bond portfolio before. Just to make sure we know where we are, let's go over the reasons for our biggest positions."

Table 7.1 Portfolio Appraisal With Yield to Worst: Nuclear Winter Corporate Bonds—All Portfolios

Settlement Date	Face Value	Security	Coupon	Maturity	Purchase Price	Total Cost	% of Assets	Yield to Maturity	Yield to Worst	Modified Duration
Corporate Bonds										
09/03/10	$125,000	Healthy Body Corp.	3.750%	03/15/12	101.000	$126,250	1%	3.077%	3.077%	1.457
03/03/09	200,000	Gold Mining, Inc.	6.000%	02/15/13	98.000	196,000	2%	6.582%	6.227%	3.447
09/03/10	150,000	Big Blue	1.000%	03/15/13	99.900	149,850	2%	1.040%	1.040%	2.483
06/15/10	185,000	Lock N Load Arms Corp.	5.650%	01/15/14	98.750	182,688	2%	6.041%	6.041%	3.122
06/15/09	140,000	Operating Companies, Inc.	5.000%	01/15/14	96.000	134,400	2%	6.010%	5.737%	3.937
08/29/08	160,000	Oil Slick International	6.750%	01/25/14	95.000	152,000	2%	7.902%	7.645%	4.391
09/12/09	185,000	American Telecom	3.750%	02/15/14	98.000	181,300	2%	4.250%	4.007%	4.018
09/20/09	140,000	Laptop Computers Internat'l	5.780%	06/04/14	98.000	137,200	2%	6.275%	6.108%	3.986
09/03/10	200,000	Package Delivery International	3.800%	06/15/14	104.000	208,000	2%	2.680%	2.680%	3.491
10/01/07	190,000	AngelMed, Inc.	5.000%	09/13/14	91.000	172,900	2%	6.637%	5.814%	5.693
08/29/10	160,000	Drilling For You, Inc.	6.157%	02/15/15	96.000	153,600	2%	7.221%	7.221%	3.809
04/03/09	100,000	BioTech Logic, Inc.	4.750%	07/15/15	99.000	99,000	1%	4.936%	4.884%	5.315
09/03/10	300,000	Global Burgers Corp.	4.000%	09/03/15	107.000	321,000	4%	2.502%	2.502%	4.541
Subtotal Corp	$2,235,000					$2,214,188	25%			

"Got it written down in the comment box of each position in the automated e-workbook." Neo opened the trading binder.

Greedo could see it was bristling with yellow Post-its. "What are all those things?" he asked.

"Reminders," said Neo. "For example, this one reminds me to buy as many corporate bonds with poison puts as possible."

"What's a *poison put*?"

Neo's mouth formed a sly smile, "They're a great thing for savvy investors in a hot merger-and-acquisition market. Poison puts force redemption of the corporate bonds if there is a change in control of the company. Poison puts usually take out the affected bonds at a price of 101 percent of the face value."

"Why is that important to us?"

Neo said, "It's important because many times such acquisitions pile on more debt to finance the takeover. This could reduce the value of our bonds. Besides, we bought the current management team. We don't know anything about the acquirers. We may not want them. So I want us out at a specific price. Let's get back to the reasons why we bought each of the newly rebalanced positions."

"I'm listening," Greedo leaned back in his chair and closed his eyes. "Go."

"Gold Mining, Inc.: We have $200 grand face value as a defensive strategy.

"Package Delivery International: It's like FedEx. It's in the transportation sector. Historically they do well in up as well as down markets.

"Global Burgers: You showed me the story there. I agree.

"American Telecom: Solid company. Bond-friendly management, no debt-financed stock buybacks or acquisitions. Five billion in free cash. Plus they have a sweet deal with Laptop Computers International, also one of our holdings.

"Lock-N-Load Arms Corp.: Gun sales follow the American sentiment. City police forces are understaffed and getting worse. People want to feel safe in their own homes. Two billion in free cash. Debt coverage ratio is over 3. Debt distribution says there's only $150 million in bonds maturing ahead of our position.

"Operating Companies, Inc.: A conglomerate like Berkshire Hathaway and Leucadia National. New bond-friendly CEO was just hired. They have $1.5

billion in free cash. All their businesses seem poised to survive the nuclear winter. Ours is the next bond maturing, so there's nothing between us and the cash.

"Last one, AngelMed: This is a healthcare company with the most innovative heart monitor implant on the market. It's smaller than a pacemaker. The FDA has just approved it for sale in the United States and internationally. Anthem/Blue Cross just approved it for insurance reimbursement as a preventative device. Best decision they ever made. Sales are rising 25 percent per quarter. Free cash is $3 billion and climbing. Bond friendly management. If we were stock pickers, this is the first company I would buy."

Greedo opened his eyes and leaned forward in his chair. "Really?"

"Absolutely. The risk is over with AngelMed. It took 10 years for them to get to this place. Now they're hitting on all eight cylinders. But we must stick to our trading discipline. We're bond holders. We don't do stocks—right?"

"What about TIPS?" exclaimed Greedo, slapping his palm against his forehead. "I almost forgot."

"What about *Treasury inflation-protected securities*?" Neo countered.

"We need 'em, don't we? What happens if inflation runs rampant?

"Here's the rub with TIPS." Neo sat back in his chair, prepared to launch into a topic about which he was especially expert. "TIPS were thought to be a great way to protect an investment portfolio against inflation. Buy the TIPS bond and part of your return floats with the Consumer Price Index. A great idea. Except, it doesn't actually work that way."

"It doesn't?" asked Greedo.

"I read an article in the *Wall Street Journal* about a study of TIPS correlation with the CPI between 2002 and 2009. They concluded the correlation was just 21 percent. A correlation of 100 percent is a perfect match. When you have a correlation as low as 21 percent, it means that TIPS values don't actually track the CPI as well as everyone thought."

"*Ah*, so no TIPS, right?"

Neo looked at his brother-in-law. "Now you get it. Sure, we'll watch the TIPS. If we think we need some inflation protection, we'll jump into one of the TIPS ETFs. They're more convenient and a lot more liquid than the actual TIPS."

Three Action Steps

ACTION STEP: FIRST-MORTGAGE BONDS

Corporations issue *first-mortgage* bonds. They give investors the first lien on specific property owned by the issuing corporation. In the event of default, first-mortgage bond holders have the right to seize company property in order to secure repayment. Seizing and selling property on behalf of bond holders is rarely necessary (and would always be handled by the bond's trustees). More often, the company reorganizes and arranges payment for the bond holders, since the lien gives it no choice but to satisfy the claims.

ACTION STEP: SENIOR SECURED BONDS

Specific assets back senior secured bonds. This means that in the event of default and bankruptcy, bond holders can seize the collateral assets.

If you cannot locate first-mortgage bonds, then we feel the next best thing is senior secured debt. By being near the top of the capital structure, principal is not guaranteed, but it provides greater safety than unsecured bonds.

ACTION STEP: UNSECURED BONDS

Unsecured bonds depend on the issuer's ability to pay interest and principal. Payment of interest and principal is based only on the issuer's promise to pay. Should the issuer become bankrupt, seniority is a huge issue. First, the banks get paid. Next the senior bonds—secured, then unsecured—get first dibs on whatever is left, after attorney's fees, of course. Avoid putting unsecured bonds in your nuclear winter corporate bond portfolio.

Municipal Bonds

During the nuclear winter investors need to insulate their municipal bond portfolio from credit risk. There will be a number of municipalities that default on their bonds. Some cities and counties may declare bankruptcy. Certainly, revenue bonds issued for nonessential services are a huge risk. We do not want to hold any of these. Yield hogs like El Greedo who trade a little increased cash flow for enormous credit risk will not do well in this environment.

Increasing the credit risk may get you 50 or even 100 basis points more in yield. Depending on the number of bonds you hold, that might be $10,000, $20,000, or even $50,000. However, if just one of those bonds defaults or its issuer goes bankrupt, you've lost potentially hundreds of thousands or even millions. It makes no sense to increase credit risk.

Here is a list of the types of municipal bonds in order of risk (least risk first) that will get you through the nuclear winter:

Prerefunded Bonds

These are bonds whose principal and interest payments have already been set aside by the issuer in an escrow account for disbursement when the bonds mature. There is no risk whatsoever in these bonds as long as the escrow account has the money in SLGS (state and local government series) instruments. These are special Treasurys sold directly to the escrow accounts. Their maturities are customized to match those of the bonds being redeemed.

Don't buy any prerefunded bond whose escrow is held in anything but a SLGS instrument. We've seen some using Fannie Mae and Freddie Mac as escrow collateral. These are not good enough since we have no resolution about what the federal government will do with Fannie and Freddie. Stick with SLGSs. They provide a true guarantee.

General Obligation Bonds (GOs)

GOs have the ability to tap additional tax revenues in the event of an economic shortfall. GOs usually stand in front of most other bonds in the payment structure. Therefore, GO bond holders are the first to be paid in the event of a fiscal failure. We believe state GOs are a possible addition to your nuclear winter municipal bond portfolio.

ACTION STEP: A WORD ABOUT CALIFORNIA GOS

California's school bonds have first claim on tax revenues, *followed* by the state's GOs. If California's fortunes turn even further south, this may be a consideration to those now holding or considering buying California GOs.

As for other states' GOs, before buying check to see if that state has a constitutional amendment like California's regarding priority of payments.

Also, keep in mind that under the law a state cannot file for bankruptcy protection. Whereas, that same restriction does not extend to cities, counties, and other governmental entities. This makes a state's GO safer than a city or other GO bond.

Revenue Bonds with a Secondary Repayment Source

You may have read of these *double-barreled tax-exempt bonds* in *Marilyn Cohen's Bond Smart Investor* newsletter (www.newsletters.forbes.com/SurvivingThe BondBearMarket). These munis are somewhat of a hybrid. Not only do they have a specific revenue stream, but they are backstopped by the issuer's *full faith and creditworthiness* just as if it were a regular general obligation bond.

In the event that one of the revenue streams is compromised (such as the revenue from sales tax declines), investors still have the security provided by the alternative source of funds. A double-barrel sewer revenue bond is a good example. This is an essential service. The municipality unquestionably cannot do without it. Such bonds are funded by revenue from the sewer it built. Bond payments are further backstopped by the local tax revenues if the sewer district encounters a problem.

Because of the dual source of repayment, double-barrel bonds are safer than regular general obligation bonds. During the upcoming years we expect municipalities to struggle. As default rates rise, a double repayment source is a big plus.

However, double-barrel bonds may be hard to find. When they become available, they may be priced a little higher than other general obligation bonds because of the added safety. You will have to specifically ask your brokers to find some essential service double-barrel bonds for you.

California Economic Recovery bonds are double-barreled. They are backed by a special one-quarter-cent pledge of California's sales tax revenues. Then, if needed, they are further backed by the full faith and credit of California. Even though California's economic problems won't go away anytime soon, this alternative source of payment reassures investors and makes the bonds more marketable.

Essential Service Revenue Bonds

These are revenue bonds issued for really important infrastructure projects such as the sewers and water facilities. Because revenue from property owners who use the facilities repays these bonds, we consider them low risk. However, there can be some serious problems.

For example, be sure that the issuer is a stable, mature area where property taxes are consistent. Do not buy water and sewer bonds from a new issuer that depends on attracting new residents to a new housing development. Further, stay away from issuers whose tax base is eroding because people are being foreclosed out of their homes with no new owners in sight.

We would allocate a portion of the municipal bond portfolio to essential service bonds during the nuclear winter.

Day 14: War Room, 5:03 A.M.

Greedo walked into the War Room and saw his brother-in-law already hard at work. He put down the coffee cup he had brought for him.

"Thanks, my all-too-thoughtful relation. I'm getting ready to plot the course of our municipal bond portfolio."

"What do you have?"

Neo picked up the coffee and blew away the steam. "Okay, after the triage we did a few days ago, we're left with just seven munis. Our total investment is $1.4 million."

"*Hmmm*," said Greedo. Our allocation target is $2.2 million. We need to find another $800,000 in safe municipal bonds."

"Probably more than that. Going into the nuclear winter we want the duration of the munis to average around 4 years. Right now, it's way above that."

Greedo was impressed at Neo's quick command of their situation. "We know the issuers of the positions we currently hold. Except for those Las Vegas monorails, all of them are general obligation bonds. Let's just see if we can swap out of the maturities we now have and get into maturities no later than 2015 or so."

"On it," said Neo, punching up the Schwab and Fidelity trading screens. Let's see what's out there. Come to Papa."

■ ■ ■

For this type of trading they probably won't do many online trades. Neo wants to see whether their current positions actually do have earlier maturities that better fit their duration target. Most are probably available. Once they know what maturities they want and the CUSIP number, they'll look each one up on TRACE to see where they're trading. Greedo takes it away:

■ ■ ■

"It's always a profitable day for First Rate Securities Corp.," said the syrupy voice into Greedo's ear.

"Got some buy orders to execute."

"And good morning to you, too, Mr. Greedo. I'll see if Mr. Smith is available. And please say 'hello' to that nice Neo, will you?"

After the briefest of pauses, "Hello, this is Howie. Good to hear from you, El. I just got your email with the municipal bond portfolio. You've slimmed things down over the past few days. Sure you want to do that? Here at First Rate Securities we see the bond market really gathering steam. Now's the time to jump on board before the train of opportunity leaves the station. I just happen to have some Wrigley Field Stadium bonds—"

"Joking. You're a real funster, Howie. You've seen where rates are going and how steamed up the economy is. Bond market's headed for a nuclear winter."

"Just seeing if you were awake this morning is all, Sir."

"I'm awake," growled Greedo. "I want to shorten the duration of our current holdings to between three and four years. Get me offers close as you can to the prices I got from TRACE on that list I sent you."

"Already did, Sir. I just sent them to you and Neo. All my prices are within ten basis points of the TRACE prices you sent me."

"Wait." Greedo cupped his hand over the phone. "Neo did you get First Rate's offer sheet?"

"Just came in. His offers hit each TRACE price to within ten or so basis points."

Greedo spoke into the telephone. "Okay, lift each of those seven offers—"

"*Lift*," Neo whispered in the background. "I know what *lift* means."

Greedo scowled at his uninitiated trading partner and cupped his hand over the mouthpiece. "I need to speak on the same level as the enemy brokers," he whispered back to Neo. Then he turned his attention back to the telephone: "Send Neo the confirming executed trade prices. Then stand by. We have some more shopping to do. Oh, and Howie?"

"Yes, Sir?"

"Wrigley Field stadium bonds are nonessential revenue bonds. No one in their right mind would buy those heading into the bond market abyss as we are. And Howie, in case you don't follow baseball, the Cubbies are still at the bottom of their division and always will be. So is their ticket revenue that's supposed to pay for those bonds."

■ ■ ■

Greedo's conversation with his broker clearly placed him in the driver's seat. There was no doubt for whom the broker works. However, they should have received offers from two different brokerage firms before pulling the trigger. Ten basis points off the most recent TRACE trades were too much off the market. But, *hey*, nobody's perfect. Especially El Greedo. He was right about one thing, though: The Chicago Cubs are, and appear destined to forever be, at the bottom of their division.

Table 7.2 is the rebalanced municipal bond portfolio that now includes both the shortened maturities for the existing holdings and the new positions they just put on the books.

Most are general obligation bonds. The Kentucky Power Grid bonds are prerefunded with SLGS escrowed to maturity. Both the Austin Sewer District and the Randolph County Water District bonds are double-barrel bonds with two revenue sources for payment. Together they account for $430,000 of the municipal bond portfolio.

You've probably noticed the Las Vegas Monorail bonds are finally gone. There was nothing good about them. The bonds had defaulted. Neo elected to keep them too long because he thought they had fallen about as far as they could and there was no place to go but up. He eventually gave up and sold them.

We agree. The monorail bonds were trading flat. That means that coupons were not being paid. With a face value of $100,000, these bonds were worth about $27,250 when Greedo finally sold them for what he could get and moved on.

Table 7.2 Portfolio Appraisal With Yield to Worst: Municipal Bond Nuclear Winter Portfolio

Settlement Date	Face Value	Security	Coupon	Maturity	Purchase Price	Total Cost	% of Assets	Yield to Maturity	Yield to Worst	Modified Duration
Municipal Bonds										
08/04/10	$210,000	Lower Colo Riv Auth. TEX	4.500%	05/15/14	102.010	$214,221	2%	3.921%	1.890%	3.422
08/04/10	170,000	Mobile Cnty Ala	4.500%	06/01/14	98.818	167,991	2%	4.840%	4.623%	3.445
09/04/10	100,000	Hawkeye State GO	1.250%	06/15/14	99.000	99,000	1%	1.523%	1.523%	3.666
09/04/10	100,000	Randolph County Water District	2.250%	10/31/14	102.000	102,000	1%	1.749%	1.749%	3.929
08/04/10	125,000	Evanston IL	4.000%	01/01/15	99.250	124,063	1%	4.187%	4.106%	3.986
09/04/10	300,000	Great State GO	1.750%	03/15/15	102.000	306,000	3%	1.294%	1.294%	4.314
08/04/10	50,000	Phoenix, AZ GO bond	2.250%	07/01/15	98.760	49,380	1%	2.520%	2.520%	4.605
08/04/10	50,000	KY Power Grid	3.875%	09/04/15	105.000	52,500	1%	2.812%	2.812%	4.541
09/04/10	330,000	Austin Sewer District	5.000%	09/15/15	110.000	363,000	4%	2.852%	0.991%	4.382
08/04/10	380,000	Shelby Cnty Tenn	4.750%	03/01/16	101.000	383,800	4%	4.544%	2.979%	4.762
08/04/10	300,000	Hays TEX Cons indpt. Sch. Dist	4.000%	08/15/16	108.000	324,000	4%	2.560%	0.988%	5.285
Subtotal Muni	$2,115,000					$2,185,954	25%			

Nuclear Winter–Advantaged Investments

While the overheated economy is soaring and the bond market is stumbling along the rail-bed, investors need to insulate their bond portfolios from both interest rate risk and credit risk. We take care of the credit risk when we buy prefunded bonds that are escrowed to maturity with SLGSs. However, what have we done to reduce interest rate risk? Nothing, yet.

If interest rates rise, bond prices will tank even further. There are a number of ways to insulate at least some of the portfolio from suffering such a cataclysmic decline. Here are the instruments we recommend investors use.

Shorting the U.S. Treasury Bond

There are a number of ways to short the U.S. T-bond. For individual investors the best way is to use an exchange-traded fund. They trade just like a stock and you can get in and out whenever you wish. Many of these are volatile since they use leverage to enhance the effects of their inverse movements to the U.S. Treasury bond.

Beware that these inverse and leveraged ETFs have not been stress-tested in a bear market. They *will* move inversely. But without stress testing, we don't know if they will move commensurately with the decline in Treasury bond prices. Some of the inverse and leveraged currency and index fund ETFs have not performed in lockstep as they should have. Time will tell.

Day 16: Mitchell Fitness, 4:45 P.M.

Neo slid two more 20-pound plates onto the bar for his wannabe-body-builder brother-in-law. "Give me another 12," Neo ordered. Ignoring Greedo's grunting at the added weight, Neo said, "The first nuclear-winter-advantaged position I want to take when the market opens tomorrow is to short the U.S. Treasury bond."

After only nine reps Greedo banged the bar back into the rack with a loud *clank* and grabbed his towel. "Isn't that anti-American, shorting the U.S. Treasury market?"

They changed positions. Neo talked while he thrust the bar over his head, then down, up, then down until he had done his twelve. "*Nah*. Everybody does it. I'm going to use the ProShares Ultrashort 7-10 Year. It's an ETF that corresponds to double the inverse of the BarCap U.S. Treasury 7-10 Year

Treasury Note." He carefully racked the barbell with a polite *clink*, and then took his allotted 30-second rest.

Neo continued, "It's leveraged and produces twice the inverse movement of a declining Treasury bond. So we don't need a very large position to achieve the results we're after. Think of it as insurance. I'm putting in just 3 percent of the total bond portfolio. If rates rise, this will make up a part of what we lose in the corporates and munis." Rest time over, Neo laid back on the bench and hefted the bar overhead again.

Greedo stood by, spotting his partner. "Why just 3 percent of the bond portfolio? We have $2.2 million in cash. Why not include that in the percentage allocated, too?"

Neo finished, then *clink*ed the barbell back in its rack and sat up. "*Ah-ha!* The teacher has now become the student. The reason is that cash has a duration of zero. We hedge only the duration-sensitive components of the portfolio. That means just the corporates and the munis."

Greedo said, "I get it. Let interest rates rise. We got protection."

"Yeah, well not that much protection. There are some other things we need to do."

Floating Rate Funds

Unlike the inverse ETFs, floating rate funds ride the rise in interest rates. Rather than move against interest rates, they move with them. Keep in mind, though, these are funds. You can't get in and out during the trading day like you can with an ETF unless it's a closed-end floating rate fund.

There's another caution in using floaters: credit risk. The mutual fund in which you invest has purchased floating rate loans. Should the economy suddenly start sinking, the credit quality of the loans in the fund becomes critically important. If the company issuing these loans encounters difficulty, the entire investment could go south.

■ ■ ■

The two stood 15 feet apart. Greedo hefted a 20-pound dead-ball overhead with both hands, then bounced it once to Neo. Back and forth their rhythm went as the heavy ball slammed into the rubber mat, and then slammed again on its return trip.

"I also want to put us into three floaters," Neo said. "It's not insurance like shorting the T-bond. Instead, we're actually using a rise in interest rates to our advantage. As rates rise, our return will rise along with it." *Slam.*

"How much should we allocate?" asked Greedo. *Slam.*

"About nine percent of the total portfolio. But I want to spread it evenly between three funds—the Fidelity Floating Rate High Income Fund; the Oppenheimer Senior Floating Rate; and the Blackrock Global Floating Rate Income Trust Fund." *Slllaaam.*

Greedo staggered backwards on that one. "How much will we invest for all three?" *Slam.*

"I'd like to get us about $900,000 worth of them." *Slam.*

End-Date Bond ETFs

Their name says it all. *End-date* ETFs expire at a specific future date. This way, investors can control the duration of their portfolio, and therefore, the volatility in value as rates move. Also, since it's an ETF, you don't have to worry about the time it takes to trade and the spreads. Adjustments to a portfolio's duration can be very precise using end-dated ETFs.

■ ■ ■

Staying on the same mat, Greedo and Neo sat down, feet facing one another. Neo held the 20-pound dead-ball overhead, then tossed it to Greedo who caught it, went flat, then ab-crunched up and tossed it back to Neo who did the same thing. Back and forth they went.

"What else you want to do?" asked Greedo with a gasp.

"I want to get some added precision with our bond ladders. I'm going to put 2 percent in the iShares Municipal Series and 2 percent in the Guggenheim BulletShares Corporate Bond ETF. *Ooompf.*"

"How far out for both? *Gasp.*"

Neo said, "I'll buy each of the series for four years. That pegs our duration right where we want it. *Ooompf.*"

■ ■ ■

Also realize that CMTs may be hard to find. Get your brokers to locate several fitting your parameters.

■ ■ ■

Neo tightened the flexible waist harness and handed Greedo the "reins."

"Let 'er rip," said Greedo, bracing himself. His overly disciplined partner began running against the rubber stretch cords Greedo used to hold him back.

ACTION STEP: AVOID OVERLAPPING CMTS

Make sure any constant maturing treasurys (CMTs) that you buy do not overlap with the same issuer already in your portfolio. That could create an undue concentration in that particular issuer. For example, let's say you've allocated your maximum 5 percent of the portfolio to Sallie Mae corporate bonds. Then you put in a 3 percent tranch of Sallie Mae CMTs. Suddenly, you have 8 percent of the portfolio invested in Sallie Mae. instead, just buy a different CMT, say the Morgan Stanley CMT. It has the same effect but preserves your maximum asset allocation discipline.

"I've been doing some research of my own," Greedo called forward as he struggled to keep Neo running in place. "I want to take a position in some Sallie Mae CMTs." Neo suddenly stopped running and looked back, eyebrows arched. "Don't be so surprised," Greedo said. "You owe me another 25 seconds. Get going," Greedo commanded. "Here's what I'm thinking. The Sallies pay 3 percent minimum no matter how far rates fall. Now that's below my target of 4 percent. But, here's what makes up for it. If rates rise—and I think they will—this issue pays 85 percent of the 10-year CMT, rather than just 80 percent."

Neo staggered to a stop and ripped off the Velcro waist harness. He stood facing Greedo, hands on knees, catching his breath. "Great idea, my soon-to-be-exhausted partner." He handed Greedo the harness. "Your turn."

Greedo fastened the harness around his waist. "I want to put in 20 percent of our nuclear-winter-advantaged portfolio into these."

"I'll do it first thing in the morning," said Neo. "*Mush.*"

LEAPS

Long-term equity anticipation securities (LEAPS) are really options. We're most interested in the LEAPS options on U.S. Treasury securities. Investors use this type of LEAPS for three purposes:

1. To profit from a rise in interest rates.
2. To profit from a fall in interest rates.
3. To establish a floor below which value will not fall.

The advantage of using interest rate LEAPS is that you can accomplish your strategy with much less capital outlay since you're buying an option rather than ponying up for the actual security.

■ ■ ■

Greedo collapsed on the mat in a puddle of sweat. "Nicely done," said Neo, dropping the reins. "Almost finished—10 minutes of stretching, then we're outta' here."

Greedo rolled over on his towel. "While you were flogging me, I remembered another hedge I read about—LEAPS."

"I thought they were just for stocks," said Neo, grabbing his left foot and bending his leg backward and up toward the ceiling.

"Actually, no. They have interest rate LEAPS. Since we don't know how long this nuclear winter will last, these contracts are for longer terms. I want to use the LEAPS to beef up our yield when rates rise. We buy a LEAPS call. As rates rise, the contract becomes more valuable. So we have hedged part of our bond portfolio from further decline."

Neo stood on the blue half-dome bosu ball, then balanced on one foot and bent forward, thrusting the free leg backward until it was parallel to the mat with both arms out from his side like airplane wings. He stood there serenely balancing motionless with just one foot on the unstable platform. "Perfect," he said. "If we can do that, then we might also buy a put option to create a floor and limit our downside risk." Neo was a quick study.

Rebalanced Portfolio for the Nuclear Winter

With their portfolio newly rebalanced for the nuclear winter, the two investors have accomplished a number of things. First, they have removed much of the credit risk that comes from the uncertain municipal credit market. They have created a more stable corporate bond portfolio by moving into blue-chip issues. They have also hedged some of their downside risk with a number of easy-to-implement tools. Here's how our two traders view their rebalancing efforts:

Day 21: War Room, 4:44 P.M.

Neo sat back in his chair, holding up a sheaf of computer reports. "Here we are, El. I have all the reports that show our new portfolio rebalanced to survive the nuclear winter."

"Across all the trading platforms and brokerages we use? How'd you do that?"

"Yep. My automated e-workbook consolidates all our positions from each of the brokerage accounts we use—"

"How much did that automated e-workbook cost us? Five grand?" Greedo groused.

"Actually, it was free. Well, I had to the buy this book to get the automated e-workbook. Anyway, look here. This report shows all positions divided by security type." He handed over the report. [See Portfolio Appraisal Report on pages 119-121].

"*Hmmm*," said Greedo, looking over the rows of numbers that represented his family's financial future. "Corporates look right at $2.2 million. Munis are okay, too. Cash and Other Securities is 50 percent of the portfolio. I see you got my LEAPS right." He looked across the desk at Neo. "I am impressed. We've really brought the duration down to 4.1—a level that won't allow a spike in interest rates to kill us."

Neo nodded. "Look at my asset allocation report." He handed the colorful pie-chart over to Greedo.

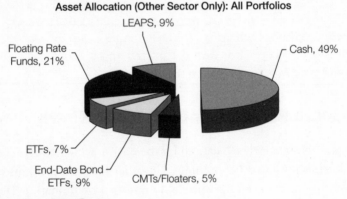

Asset Allocation (Other Sector Only): All Portfolios

LEAPS, 9%
Cash, 49%
Floating Rate Funds, 21%
ETFs, 7%
End-Date Bond ETFs, 9%
CMTs/Floaters, 5%

Asset Allocations Other Sector

"This shows the special positions we put on just to hedge against the nuclear winter. See how we kept almost half in cash and other securities as dry powder? We allocated the $2.2 million to the advantaged securities that will save our butts as the economy gets worse." Neo passed a second pie-chart to Greedo.

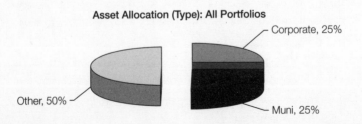

Asset Allocation (Type): All Portfolios

Corporate, 25%
Other, 50%
Muni, 25%

Portfolio Appraisal Report

Portfolio Appraisal With Yield to Worst: Nuclear Winter All Portfolios Rebalanced

Settlement Date	Face Value	Security	Coupon	Maturity	Purchase Price	Total Cost	% of Assets	Yield to Maturity	Yield to Worst	Modified Duration
Corporate Bonds										
09/03/10	$125,000	Healthy Body Corp.	3.750%	03/15/12	101.000	$126,250	1%	3.077%	3.077%	1.457
03/03/09	200,000	Gold Mining, Inc.	6.000%	02/15/13	98.000	196,000	2%	6.582%	6.227%	3.447
09/03/10	150,000	Big Blue	1.000%	03/15/13	99.900	149,850	2%	1.040%	1.040%	2.483
06/15/10	185,000	Lock N Load Arms Corp.	5.650%	01/15/14	98.750	182,688	2%	6.041%	6.041%	3.122
06/15/09	140,000	Operating Companies, Inc.	5.000%	01/15/14	96.000	134,400	2%	6.010%	5.737%	3.937
08/29/08	160,000	Oil Slick International	6.750%	01/25/14	95.000	152,000	2%	7.902%	7.645%	4.391
09/12/09	185,000	American Telecom	3.750%	02/15/14	98.000	181,300	2%	4.250%	4.007%	4.018
09/20/09	140,000	Laptop Computers Internat'l	5.780%	06/04/14	98.000	137,200	2%	6.275%	6.108%	3.986
09/03/10	200,000	Package Delivery International	3.800%	06/15/14	104.000	208,000	2%	2.680%	2.680%	3.491
10/01/07	190,000	AngelMed, Inc.	5.000%	09/13/14	91.000	172,900	2%	6.637%	5.814%	5.693
08/29/10	160,000	Drilling For You, Inc.	6.157%	02/15/15	96.000	153,600	2%	7.221%	7.221%	3.809
04/03/09	100,000	BioTech Logic, Inc.	4.750%	07/15/15	99.000	99,000	1%	4.936%	4.884%	5.315
09/03/10	300,000	Global Burgers Corp.	4.000%	09/03/15	107.000	321,000	4%	2.502%	2.502%	4.541
Subtotal Corp	$2,235,000					$2,214,188	25%			

(Continued)

Portfolio Appraisal With Yield to Worst: Nuclear Winter All Portfolios Rebalanced (Continued)

Settlement Date	Face Value	Security	Coupon	Maturity	Purchase Price	Total Cost	% of Assets	Yield to Maturity	Yield to Worst	Modified Duration
Municipal Bonds										
08/04/10	$210,000	Lower Colo Riv Auth. TEX	4.500%	05/15/14	102.010	$214,221	2%	3.921%	1.890%	3.422
08/04/10	170,000	Mobile Cnty Ala	4.500%	06/01/14	98.818	167,991	2%	4.840%	4.623%	3.445
09/04/10	100,000	Hawkeye State GO	1.250%	06/15/14	99.000	99,000	1%	1.523%	1.523%	3.666
09/04/10	100,000	Randolph County Water District	2.250%	10/31/14	102.000	102,000	1%	1.749%	1.749%	3.929
08/04/10	125,000	Evanston IL	4.000%	01/01/15	99.250	124,063	1%	4.187%	4.106%	3.986
09/04/10	300,000	Great State GO	1.750%	03/15/15	102.000	306,000	3%	1.294%	1.294%	4.314
08/04/10	50,000	Phoenix, AZ GO bond	2.250%	07/01/15	98.760	49,380	1%	2.520%	2.520%	4.605
08/04/10	50,000	KY Power Grid	3.875%	09/04/15	105.000	52,500	1%	2.812%	2.812%	4.541
09/04/10	330,000	Austin Sewer District	5.000%	09/15/15	110.000	363,000	4%	2.852%	0.991%	4.382
08/04/10	380,000	Shelby Cnty Tenn	4.750%	03/01/16	101.000	383,800	4%	4.544%	2.979%	4.762
08/04/10	300,000	Hays TEX Cons indpt. Sch. Dist	4.000%	08/15/16	108.000	324,000	4%	2.560%	0.988%	5.285
Subtotal Muni	$2,115,000					$2,185,954	25%			
Subtotal bond portfolio only						$4,400,142	50%			
Average Weighted Yields for bond portfolio only								3.969%	3.372%	

Average Weighted Duration for bond portfolio only 4.100

Other Securities

Date	Par	Name			Price	Market Value	%			
10/12/10	$2,175,000	Schwab Money Market Fund	N/A	N/A	100.000	$2,175,000	25%	N/A	N/A	N/A
10/12/10	300,000	Black Rock Global Floating Rate Income Trust	N/A	N/A	100.000	300,000	3%	N/A	N/A	N/A
10/12/10	200,000	iShares Municipal Series	N/A	N/A	100.000	200,000	2%	N/A	N/A	N/A
10/12/10	200,000	Claymore Bullet Shares Corporate Bond ETF	N/A	N/A	100.000	200,000	2%	N/A	N/A	N/A
10/12/10	300,000	Fidelity Floating Rate High Income Fund	N/A	N/A	100.000	300,000	3%	N/A	N/A	N/A
10/12/10	200,000	Sallie Mae CMTs	N/A	N/A	100.000	200,000	2%	N/A	N/A	N/A
10/12/10	300,000	Oppenhiemer Senior Floating Rate	N/A	N/A	100.000	300,000	3%	N/A	N/A	N/A
10/12/10	300,000	ProShares Ultra Short 7-10 Year ETF	N/A	N/A	100.000	300,000	3%	N/A	N/A	N/A
10/12/10	400,000	LEAPS	N/A	N/A	100.000	400,000	5%	N/A	N/A	N/A
Subtotal Other Securities	$4,375,000					$4,375,000	50%			
Total Portfolio						$8,775,142	100.0%			

"See how we executed our plan of allocating 25 percent each to corporates and munis, then the rest to cash and the hedges?"

El Greedo respectfully put down the report. "Can you show me how much a shift in interest rates will affect us?"

Neo's fingers flew across the keyboard. The printer erupted with the Sensitivity Report. "This shows how varying changes in interest rates—up or down—will impact the portfolio we built," he said. [See Sensitivity Report on pages 123-125].

Greedo scanned the columns of numbers, then threw back his big bald head and laughed. "Well, my-sister's-too-brilliant husband, I guess we did it. A move of as much as 150 basis points either up or down produces profits or losses of just 3 percent or less in the bonds we own. We got us the armor-plated portfolio we intended. I can live with that until this nuclear winter ends."

■ ■ ■

One other thing El didn't mention was the distribution of assets not only across various asset classes, but within the classes, across a wide variety of securities. No single position—except cash—accounts for more than 5 percent of the total portfolio. Indeed, that 5 percent is just one position—the LEAPS. The next highest is four percent (just four positions) or less.

Now that we know how to insulate the investment portfolio from the nuclear winter, there's another dangerous occurrence that can bite you—credit risk in the municipal bond market. Chapter 8 shows you just what to watch for and how to deal with it.

Sensitivity Report

Portfolio Sensitivity Nuclear Winter Bond Portfolios Only

Settlement Date	Face Value	Security	Coupon	Maturity	Purchase Price	Total Cost	Yield to Worst	Call Price	Δ in Value -150 bps	Δ in Value -100 bps	Δ in Value -50 bps	Δ in Value +50 bps	Δ in Value +100 bps	Δ in Value +150 bps
Corporate Bonds														
09/03/10	$125,000	Healthy Body Corp.	3.750%	03/15/12	101.000	$126,250	3.077%	100.000	$2,849	$1,890	$940	($931)	($1,853)	($2,765)
03/03/09	200,000	Gold Mining, Inc.	6.000%	02/15/13	98.000	196,000	6.227%	100.000	13,072	9,448	5,900	(978)	(4,312)	(7,577)
09/03/10	150,000	Big Blue	1.000%	03/15/13	99.900	149,850	1.040%	100.000	0	3,796	1,883	(1,855)	(3,683)	(5,484)
06/15/10	185,000	Lock N Load Arms Corp.	5.650%	01/15/14	98.750	182,688	6.041%	100.000	9,017	5,953	2,948	(2,892)	(5,728)	(8,511)
06/15/09	140,000	Operating Companies, Inc.	5.000%	01/15/14	96.000	134,400	5.737%	100.000	10,001	7,094	4,256	(1,221)	(3,863)	(6,443)
08/29/08	160,000	Oil Slick International	6.750%	01/25/14	95.000	152,000	7.645%	100.000	12,383	8,739	5,192	(1,621)	(4,894)	(8,080)
09/12/09	185,000	American Telecom	3.750%	02/15/14	98.000	181,300	4.007%	100.000	13,275	9,355	5,527	(1,864)	(5,431)	(8,915)
09/20/09	140,000	Laptop Computers Internat'l	5.780%	06/04/14	98.000	137,200	6.108%	100.000	9,662	6,682	3,773	(1,837)	(4,541)	(7,182)
09/03/10	200,000	Package Delivery International	3.800%	06/15/14	104.000	208,000	2.680%	100.000	11,328	7,473	3,698	(3,622)	(7,170)	(10,646)

(Continued)

Portfolio Sensitivity Nuclear Winter Bond Portfolios Only (Continued)

Settlement Date	Face Value	Security	Coupon	Maturity	Purchase Price	Total Cost	Yield to Worst	Call Price	Δ in Value -150 bps	Δ in Value -100 bps	Δ in Value -50 bps	Δ in Value +50 bps	Δ in Value +100 bps	Δ in Value +150 bps
10/01/07	190,000	AngelMed, Inc.	5.000%	09/13/14	91.000	172,900	5.814%	100.000	24,851	19,162	13,666	3,222	(1,738)	(6,532)
08/29/10	160,000	Drilling For You, Inc.	6.157%	02/15/15	96.000	153,600	7.221%	100.000	9,110	6,003	2,967	(2,900)	(5,733)	(8,503)
04/03/09	100,000	BioTech Logic, Inc.	4.750%	07/15/15	99.000	99,000	4.884%	100.000	8,667	5,780	2,983	(2,352)	(4,895)	(7,361)
09/03/10	300,000	Global Burgers Corp.	4.000%	09/03/15	107.000	321,000	2.502%	100.000	22,757	14,970	7,386	(7,193)	(14,200)	(21,025)
Subtotal Corp	$2,235,000					$2,214,188			$146,973	$106,345	$61,119	($26,043)	($68,041)	($109,024)
Municipal Bonds														
08/04/10	$210,000	Lower Colo Riv Auth. TEX	4.500%	05/15/14	102.010	$214,221	1.890%	100.000	$28,134	$23,896	$19,744	$11,696	$7,795	$3,973
08/04/10	170,000	Mobile Cnty Ala	4.500%	06/01/14	98.818	167,991	4.623%	100.000	10,384	7,285	4,250	(1,636)	(4,489)	(7,285)

09/04/10	100,000	Hawkeye State GO	1.250%	06/15/14	99.000	99,000	1.523%	100.000	5,636	3,718	1,839	(1,801)	(3,564)	(5,291)
09/04/10	100,000	Randolph County Water District	2.250%	10/31/14	102.000	102,000	1.749%	100.000	6,269	4,131	2,042	(1,996)	(3,947)	(5,855)
08/04/10	125,000	Evanston IL	4.000%	01/01/15	99.250	124,063	4.106%	100.000	8,148	5,506	2,925	(2,058)	(4,463)	(6,813)
09/04/10	300,000	Great State GO	1.750%	03/15/15	102.000	306,000	1.294%	100.000	0	13,644	6,737	(6,573)	(12,986)	(19,243)
08/04/10	50,000	Phoenix, AZ GO bond	2.250%	07/01/15	98.760	49,380	2.520%	100.000	3,557	2,340	1,155	(1,125)	(2,220)	(3,287)
08/04/10	50,000	KY Power Grid	3.875%	09/04/15	105.000	52,500	2.812%	100.000	3,781	2,487	1,227	(1,194)	(2,357)	(3,490)
09/04/10	330,000	Austin Sewer District	5.000%	09/15/15	110.000	363,000	0.991%	102.000	0	0	47,291	29,049	20,285	11,750
08/04/10	380,000	Shelby Cnty Tenn	4.750%	03/01/16	101.000	383,800	2.979%	100.000	62,476	51,516	40,869	20,474	10,708	1,217
08/04/10	300,000	Hays TEX Cons indpt. Sch. Dist	4.000%	08/15/16	108.000	324,000	0.988%	102.000	0	0	44,359	24,795	15,464	6,419
Subtotal Muni	$2,115,000					$2,185,954			$128,385	$114,521	$172,438	$69,632	$20,224	($27,904)
Total Bond Portfolio						$4,400,142			$275,358	$220,866	$233,557	$43,589	($47,817)	($136,928)

Chapter 8
MUNI BOND CREDIT FAMINE

Why spend time trying to understand the coming municipal bond credit crisis? Simple: Without a working understanding of municipal credit, you are at the mercy of others in interpreting what's happening to you. The media usually run with a story—right or wrong—just to fill air time. The elected officials who cause these credit problems haven't a clue (or a care, it seems) about the ramifications of their decisions in the financial markets. The brokers and bond salespeople you talk with will twist the truth just to get you to buy a bond. At the end of the day, the only judgment you can trust is your own.

The biggest worry bond holders should have as we head into a municipal credit famine is accidentally overconcentrating in a particular issue, city, county, or state. Here's how it happens:

Day 14: War Room, 5:45 A.M.

"So, my overconcentrating kin, I see you really like Texas."

Greedo tossed another log into the War Room's fireplace and said, "Texas is a good state to issue munis. But I don't have more affection for Texas than I do for any other state."

Neo shuffled his papers and held up a pie-chart for Greedo to see. "This report says different. Looky here."

Greedo stepped from the warmth toward the desk and peered at the page. "What's that you got?"

"This is our Asset Allocations by Region for all of our portfolio positions across all of our trading platforms. I printed it right from the e-workbook. We have 11 percent of our wealth concentrated in Texas in one form or another. Tennessee is the next highest at 4 percent."

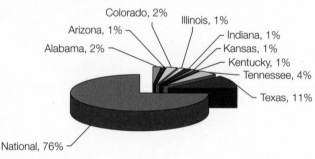

Asset Allocations by Region

Greedo snatched the paper from Neo's fingers. "You sure? I just looked at the Schwab statement. It said we just had 3 percent of our money in Texas."

"Right. But we have accounts at several brokerage firms. And we could be in bond funds that hold assets in Texas. That adds even more to our Texas concentration."

■ ■ ■

We wouldn't criticize Greedo for owning Texas debt. We like Texas. Nor would we say that 11 percent in any given state—even one the quality of Texas—is necessarily an overconcentration.

Greedo's mistake is that he didn't know. Understanding your asset allocation by region, by sector, and by type is so important. As municipal credit

ACTION STEP: IF YOU MUST OVERCONCENTRATE

Everyone has a different philosophy about the maximum percentage of the portfolio to put in any given municipality or state. Due to the tax advantages for residents, keeping a substantial percentage of the municipal bond portfolio within your residential state's borders is sometimes a sound strategic move.

However, check out the credit status of the municipality and the state. If you make the decision to overweight the portfolio there, then you must diversify your holdings among a good number of bonds and bond types. For example, we wouldn't advise putting 50 percent of the total portfolio just in California general obligation bonds. Instead, spread it around to various bond types, essential service issues, revenue districts, and so forth.

tightens, you must know where your risks lie. Knowing your asset allocations over all your brokerage accounts and being able to report it in one place gives you a leg up on most individual investors. You can find these reports in the automated e-workbook that comes with this book.

It's not smart to put too many eggs in any municipality basket when it appears that credit is becoming tight. First, they may be unable to float future bonds at an affordable rate. Second, some municipalities have overspent to the point where they need credit just to pay current bills. Among those due bills is the interest owed from prior bond issues. If the markets run away from them and they cannot get credit, the bond holders risk a default.

Unfunded Pensions and Other Social Disruptions

When we wrote this book the foreign debt crisis was in full swing. Greeks were rioting in the streets of Athens; their unions were adamant in their refusal to negotiate concessions of any kind. Ireland was begging the European Union for a bailout. The global financial markets were in turmoil.

Fulminating beneath all this were the U.S. states, cities, and counties. They all had committed the same egregious errors as so many nanny states like Greece, Portugal, Spain, and others. This error is due in large part to unfunded pension liabilities and too many giveaways that turned into permanent entitlements. The countries, states, counties, and cities simply have too many mouths to feed who no longer produce revenue.

Nanny-State Mentality

A *nanny state* is a governmental body that promises to do everything for its citizens for as long as they both shall live. So, many nanny states, like Greece, and too many municipal issuers in the United States still refuse to cut their budgets. They've made promises they cannot afford to keep.

Denial seems to be the mindset of the moment. The politicos that make the fiscal decisions seem more interested in pandering to the special-interest groups that got them elected than in serving their broader constituency.

This denial of the cash flow problem created by promised pension benefits and other excesses has caused a massive overhang of unfunded liabilities. The municipalities simply don't have the cash to pay the required amount into their employee pension and retirement funds when it comes due. So, they let it slide until next year, when things will be better, then the next year, and so on. Problem is, the next year they were counting on to be better, never is.

And so the unfunded pension liability grows. It now threatens the financial future of those states and municipalities that continue to paper-over the fiscal hole they're digging for themselves by issuing more debt.

The State of New Jersey is an example. Former Governor Jon Corzine directed his state to contribute in 2009 just $105 million to the State's public sector employee pension fund. The correct amount as determined by the State's actuaries should have been $2.3 billion. This created an unfunded pension liability shortfall of $2.29 billion. And that was just for 2009.

Governor Corzine didn't have the money to put into New Jersey's pension system. He is not alone. Nationwide estimates of the total unfunded pension liability in the United States run anywhere from $1 trillion to $3 trillion and more. No one knows for sure. The estimate depends on several forecast assumptions such as the investment return on the State's pension fund. Some states deliberately use absurd return rates—8 percent seems to be a popular number—when lowballing their unfunded pension gap.

 **ACTION STEP: UNFUNDED PENSION LIABILITY LOWERS CREDIT RATINGS**

Watch for your bond issuer's unfunded pension liability growing out of control. This will eventually compromise the issuer's ability to timely pay bond interest and repay bond principal. At a minimum, it will lower the issuer's credit rating, making it more expensive to issue additional bonds to keep their sinking ship afloat for one more election.

Contributing Factors

The chickens have come home to roost for municipalities' excesses. Three errors caused the tremendous financial problem of unfunded pension liabilities:

1. The type of pension plans granted to public sector employees.
2. The public sector employees unions that lobbied and contributed mightily to lawmaker's electoral campaigns.
3. Employees gaming the system.

Each of these is something you must understand when deciding to either add a new municipal bond to your portfolio collection or to keep a bond in the collection as interest rates begin their relentless rise.

Type of Pension Plans

We're interested in just two general types of public employee pension plans: The COLA (cost-of-living adjustment) variety and the defined-benefit variety (with determined benefits no matter what). Before the fiscal problems came to light, most retired public employees received a cost-of-living adjustment to their pension plan benefits. This moving target makes it impossible to estimate the future funds needed to pay all these people. Further, many of these plans contain health-care coverage of the Rolls Royce variety. Such plans are like a fiscal cancer that grows on the municipalities' balance sheets until it chokes off all disposable funds.

Defined-benefit plans, on the other hand, spell out the annual payout to beneficiaries. This makes the pension liability problem that much more manageable. It is true that many problem municipalities have switched to defined-benefit pension plans for their *current and future* employees. However, this does nothing to fix the problem created by the millions of public-sector employees getting benefits and annual increases from prior years and decades.

Unions—The Tail that Wags the Dog

Public employee labor unions excuse their excess behavior and the sweetheart labor contracts they negotiate by claiming they're just serving their constituency. At election time, their people answer the phones for politicians sympathetic to their cause. They contribute lavishly to specific candidates' campaigns. Their lobbyists do everything within the law (and sometimes outside it) to make legislators and officials beholden to them.

ACTION STEP: ONE CAUSE OF UNFUNDED PENSIONS

"Our policy is we don't want to cross a picket line," so said Obama White House spokesman, Robert Gibbs, of the Administration's decision to honor the Firefighter's Union's demand they boycott the Rhode Island Council of Mayors meeting in 2009. The White House was really just ensuring organized labor's continued endorsement.

It is the power of such unions as the International Association of Firefighters that holds a gun to our elected officials' heads. With over 300,000 voting members, the IAFF wields a mighty sword against politicians with the naïve fortitude to insist they back down from their contract demands.

Spending by U.S. cities will outstrip revenue by $83 billion through 2012, says the National League of Cities. A major contributor to this excess is the public employees' unions holding contracts the cities can no longer afford.

Everyone likes the firefighters. We like the firefighters. After 9/11 they are true American heroes. However, their unions have negotiated thousands of their retired members' unaffordable pay packages. Miami is an example. In a city with a median annual income of less than $30,000, 115 of its 669 firefighters made more than $150,000 during fiscal 2010 according to City figures.

To free up cash to pay their retired firefighters, some cities—Los Angeles, Philadelphia, and Milwaukee, to name just three—have resorted to temporarily closing fire stations and removing fire trucks from service. Such measures put the majority at risk for the benefit of just a few. American cities simply cannot afford such largesse.

A sweetheart deal that made news occurred in Illinois. The police officers' union negotiated a longevity pay increase for the pension benefits paid to officers with 12 or more years of service. This longevity boost increased these old timers' pay between 4 and 5 percent on top of the other negotiated pension increases.

The result of the unions' effort has been to create ironclad pension plans that strongly favor the public-sector employees at the taxpayers' fiscal peril. It is no wonder a conflict of interest exists—the legislators who sign these unrealistic pension contracts into law usually receive the same lucrative retirement provisions that other public-sector employees do.

Those administrators who are subject to independently negotiated contracts are not entirely out of the game, either. They use the public-sector employee contracts as a base from which to negotiate upward their own pension plans so they can feed from an even larger trough during retirement.

Employees Gaming the System

Small wonder that municipalities cannot afford to fund their employee pension plans. And so many people wonder why these municipalities are worried about being able to borrow the money they need to stay afloat.

Many retired employees make more in retirement compensation than they ever did as active employees. They do this by *gaming* the system. Here's how it's done:

Many pension contracts compute annual payouts based on the salary of the past year of service or the highest of the past several years. Savvy employees will *spike* their pay during these key periods by working enormous amounts of overtime and accumulating vacation and sick time prior to retirement. They do anything to increase that final key pension computation period's income amount. In some police and fire departments it is customary for the junior people to withdraw from overtime opportunities so that it goes to the senior people (whose retirement time is coming) in order to beef up that final year of income.

Some will also double-dip by retiring from their regular job, then returning as an independent, paid consultant, doing much the same work they did as an active employee. We have heard of a retired fire chief in San Ramon, CA, who managed to raise his retirement paycheck from $221,000 a year to $284,000 by using these income-spiking methods. That's an increase of 28 percent without even including cost-of-living increases.

ACTION STEP: KNOW THE TYPE OF PENSION PLAN

Because the problem of unfunded pension liability is so critical, many bond analysts are drilling down into the pension plan contract itself. They want to know the nature of any scheduled increases and unusual things— like the police officers' longevity increase described above. Ask your broker for an analyst's report of the underfunded pension problems related to your municipal bond holdings.

Swaps: Another Nail in the Municipal Coffin

We hope every municipal debt investor has heard of *interest rate swaps*. In their desperate search for quick cash, cities and other municipal debt issuers put themselves into these toxic swaps. The deal was pitched by Wall Street as protection for the municipal issuers in the event of a rising interest rate market. It did this by swapping floating-rate debt for fixed-rate debt. Fine in theory.

Only rates didn't go up. As a result, the municipalities were on the hook for tens of millions, and some for hundreds of millions in payments to their swap counterparties. Bloomberg reported on November 9, 2010 that public entities had paid over $4 billion to Wall Street in swaps that had backfired. This debt obligation came on top of the already-onerous unfunded pension liabilities. The house of cards so many of these municipalities created became even less sturdy.

First, and most important to the municipal treasurers, many swaps gave them immediate, up-front cash payments for doing the deal. Often these were worth many millions. They thought it was manna from heaven. It ended up being Wall Street's Trojan horse.

The swap mania wasn't limited to cities. The smartest people in the room got caught in swaps. Cornell University, for example, paid $39.9 million to terminate bond swaps of $475 million in municipal bonds it issued. As a result, Standard & Poor's cut Cornell's credit rating to AA. Moody's analysts, Kimberly Tuby and Dennis Gephardt, issued a similar downgrading report that cited a "thinner cushion for a significant amount of debt and large expense base."

Harvard University paid a whopping $925 million to terminate $1.9 billion in wrong-way swaps. The oldest and richest of America's universities (with an endowment of over $20 billion) appealed to Massachusetts to fast-track their next $2.5 billion borrowing.

Not to be outdone by rival Harvard, Yale University had entered into 32 separate bond swap agreements totaling $975 million. The point here is that the people running these universities' finances are the top in the industry. They supposedly understood swaps and derivatives. Their job was to know how devastating swaps could be if their bet on interest rates went against them.

The municipal treasurers who entered into the same types of toxic instruments had already struck out even before the first pitch was thrown. When Wall Street came knocking on their door with a wheelbarrow full of up-front cash to do a swap deal, they all opened wide and begged the wolf to walk into the room.

This helped create a doomsday scenario for the municipal markets. Bond issuer credit ratings have suffered. Too many have precious little money to meet current expenses. Forget about funding some pension fund for future payout. They're worried about keeping the lights on today. They have no choice but to borrow in the debt market.

However, the interest rates they will pay rose owing to their precarious financial conditions. This requires them to borrow even more—and more often—to pay the increased interest expense. The municipality's mountain of debt grows like an erupting volcano. Many will sink under its weight. We don't want your portfolio to be among them.

Drowning in Debt Obligations

Municipal bond issuers—states, cities, and counties—cannot catch up with their pension funding and other financial liabilities. As we write this, the infamous Jefferson County, Alabama, appointed a receiver and hovers on the brink of what could be the largest municipal bankruptcy in U.S. history due to interest rate swaps—surpassing the 1994 bankruptcy of Orange County, CA.

However, Orange County filed for bankruptcy for a completely different reason. They lost a huge amount of money from leveraged investments.

The problem was a one-off event that was repaired. That's not the situation now. Today, the unfunded liabilities, swap contracts, declining tax revenues, and elected legislators unwilling to cut expenses for fear of being thrown out of office by special interests are a systemic problem affecting the entire U.S. municipal debt structure. It is a *structural* rather than a *cyclical* problem. Cyclical problems go away when the cycle ends; structural problems are there forever.

Los Angeles is one of several major cities under the microscope. LA has unfunded pension liabilities of $2.3 billion but a budget shortfall equal to 10 percent of the entire budget. Los Angeles will not catch up with its pension liabilities any time soon.

Former LA Mayor Richard Riordan stated in a *Wall Street Journal* article that bankruptcy was Los Angeles's only way out of its financial dilemma. To us, it seems almost a footrace between Los Angeles and San Diego, CA—equally unsteady—as to which will pull the bankruptcy ripcord first.

One thing is for sure: Whichever big city does declare itself bankrupt, there will be a flood of others to follow. City councils across the country are watching to see what relief from their huge liabilities bankruptcy affords. So far, small cities that have gone bankrupt have not attempted to cancel retirement pension obligations. Nor have many cut public-sector staff in an attempt to reduce costs.

The Fallacy of Bankruptcy

For municipalities in 26 states, filing for bankruptcy is just wishful thinking. By statute, these 26 states prohibit their municipalities from filing for bankruptcy protection. To do so, the afflicted municipality would have to sue to enact a specific statute allowing it to file. This would be enormously expensive and would probably take years to wind through the courts. By the time a verdict was rendered, the municipality would long ago have run out of money.

If you own municipal bonds issued by entities within these states, you probably don't need to worry about them going bankrupt because they can't. They'll just issue more debt and continue limping along. Should the credit markets lock them out (unlikely, but it could happen to some), they will simply default on their bonds. They may just stop paying the interest coupons

States Prohibiting Municipal Bankruptcy

Alaska	Delaware	Georgia
Hawaii	Illinois	Indiana
Iowa	Kansas	Maine
Maryland	Massachusetts	Mississippi
Nevada	New Hampshire	New Mexico
North Dakota	Oregon	Rhode Island
South Dakota	Tennessee	Utah
Vermont	Virginia	Wisconsin
Wyoming		

or restructure their debt by decreasing the coupons and extending maturities. When principal payment time comes along, they could default on that payment, too.

Historically, bond holders are usually made whole. However, it usually takes considerable time and the ultimate result is often to the detriment of the bond holders.

Since municipalities need the debt market for a continuous stream of new money, most will attempt to work out an arrangement with their bond holders before actually defaulting.

China Syndrome of Municipal Defaults

Everyone is watching for that first major city bankruptcy test case. They're wondering what kind of a deal with bond holders the municipality can cut. That first deal will serve as a benchmark for the flood of others we're certain will follow.

Whether the first big city just defaults on its bond debt or actually seeks protection under Chapter 9 of the U.S. Bankruptcy Code in an attempt to extinguish certain of their liabilities, it will cause a burning tumult in the municipal bond market.

Individual investors will panic, looking at their bond portfolios as being at risk of default. They will sell *en masse*. The municipal bond market will see a selling panic like none other in history. Bond prices will plunge, sinking all boats with it.

Day 15: Lady Alice Cleaners, 6:46 A.M.

Greedo walked up to the counter and put down his laundry ticket.

"*Ahh*, good morning, Mista Greedo. I hear you are having second thoughts about selling those San Alita GOs."

"Huh?" asked Greedo. "What do you know about San Alita?"

"*Ahh*, Mista Neo and I talk when he drop off laundry. May a humble dry cleaner offer some advice?" Greedo saw the man's face go hard with conviction. "No second thoughts on any trades. None. Ever. Selling San Alita was a brilliant call. There is a municipal credit crisis coming. Even creditworthy municipalities will suffer. And San Alita certainly is less creditworthy than most of them."

"So you are a market player, too?" *Everyone is in the market*, Greedo thought. *Each thinks he's an expert.*

The man behind the counter humbly shrugged. "Only a little bit. My municipal bond portfolio is just $1 million. It is 10 percent of everything—"

Greedo did the math. *Ten million dollars? This guy's richer than me.*

"Most of my money is tied up in the other seven laundries, two Subway franchises, and a couple of apartment houses. Then there is the Mexican restaurant chain and the stock portfolio—"

"So what do you think about munis?" asked Greedo, suddenly more respectful.

The man stood straight, pleased at being asked his opinion. "I think problem extends to most municipal bond issuers. If they can issue needed debt, it will be at exorbitant rates. Bond prices plummet as yields soar. Running a city's finances under such conditions like running dry cleaner using nothing but credit card, making bare minimum payments. Debt mounts. Interest expense rises. Soon majority of every income dolla goes to pay debt." The man stopped to be sure his customer was getting all this.

"Result," he continued, "a liquidity crisis in the municipal bond market. Few buyers willing to take bonds off of any seller's hands. San Alita is going to be one of the hardest hit and among the first to go."

Greedo stood back from the counter, amazed. *Am I the only one who struggles with this stuff?* he wondered. "You know a lot about the markets. What are you doing here running a dry cleaner?"

The humble laundryman looked closely at his customer. "If I not here, who wash your clothes, Mista Greedo?"

■ ■ ■

The humble, but very savvy, dry cleaner is right. The future for municipal finances looks bleak, indeed. However, there is a way out. Chapter 9 shows how to read the tealeaves to discover the green shoots of recovery from the coming nuclear winter in the bond market.

INVESTMENT DEFICIT DISORDER

Day 227: El Burrito, Jr., 12.45 P.M.

"*Buenos dias*, Señor Greedo. How are you today?"

Greedo walked up to the ordering window of his favorite Mexican take-out lunch counter. "Today is a great day, Gustavo. My usual, if you don't mind."

"I saw you parking the Kia, Señor Greedo. My boys are already assembling your superdeluxe chicken burrito. It will be ready in three minutes. Why is today such a great day, Señor?"

Greedo leaned against the steel counter of the takeout window. Twenty years of passing the city's finest Mexican food to an adoring public had left it burnished and lustrous in the Los Angeles sunshine. "I'll tell you, Gus. This nuclear winter for investors is finally over. My indicators show that the green shoots of a turnaround have finally surfaced—"

Gustavo's eyes grew wide. "That is what you think, Señor? Green shoots? Finally prosperity in the bond markets?"

Greedo nodded his head with confidence. "Yep, that's right, Gus. I'm going all in; taking advantage of some tremendous opportunities. I've been itching for this day. Now it's finally here."

Gus hefted the white bag containing Greedo's burrito, a Diet Coke, and crispy, fried tortillas for the trip home. "But that is not what Neo says, Señor. He was here yesterday. Neo says I must be very careful. Neo fears that this is just a false start. He doesn't want me to be . . . wheeepsawed."

"Neo told you that?"

"Si, Señor."

"And you believe him?" asked Greedo.

"Of course." Gus eyed Greedo as if to say anyone would be crazy not to believe Neo. "Over the past year, I have followed Neo's advice and have saved my municipal bond portfolio several millions from stupid trades he told me not to do."

 "Several millions?"

"Si, Señor. What, you think I am just a simple *burrito-ista*? This restaurant is one of five that I own. I'm also partners with my amigo in seven dry cleaning stores and a couple of Subway shops. Then there are the apartment houses and the trailer park on the ocean. Not bad for a kid raised in Covina, huh?"

"So why do you work here?"

Gus eyeballed Greedo. "If I no work here, who would make your lunch, Señor? Say, you tell that savant of all investments you are related to 'hello' for me, *eh*? I packed him a little something to keep up his strength." Gus patted the bulging white bag and handed it across the counter to Greedo.

Symptoms of IDD

Investment deficit disorder (IDD) is an affliction suffered by millions of individual investors. Greedo certainly seems to have a nasty case. Symptoms of IDD are easy to spot among investors, but are not so easy to cure. Most suffering from IDD show symptoms such as:

- They are absolutely certain they can see the bond market's coming turnaround.

- They are equally certain that the train of general economic downturn is leaving the station. If they don't jump into bonds right now, they'll be left behind. They are wrong.

- Instead of testing the waters by investing a small percentage of their portfolio, they feel driven to put everything into what is absolutely, most certainly, and without a doubt the ground-floor beginning of the new bull market for bonds.

It is almost impossible to talk those suffering from IDD out of making ill-advised trades. They think they have all the answers. They will accuse those conducting such an intervention of trying to sabotage their economic well-being. They will accuse those who are merely trying to save the IDD victim from their own bullheadedness of wanting all the immense profits that are just around the corner for themselves. In the end, they have only themselves to blame for leaping into the fray with everything they have.

Emergence of Bull and Bear Markets

Every market change, whether it is to a bull or to a bear market, moves in an irregular, sawtooth pattern. There is no singular, defining move into the new bull or bear market. The major markets like stocks and bonds have some advances—often several—followed by quick-but-brutal pullbacks. They will keep doing this until they establish a definite trajectory. But even then there will be wiggles that unknowing traders find costly.

We know that you understand this. Everyone does—on an intellectual level. However, emotion often preempts market logic. Yield-hungry bond investors have a visceral need to put money to work. When they think the right direction has finally arrived, too often they overcommit their asset allocation at exactly the wrong time.

Market technicians make their careers tracking trends. They extrapolate them into a prediction of market direction and timing. Even they are not right most of the time.

Day 227: War Room, 1:15 P.M.

Greedo set the heavily laden, bulging white bag on his desk. Neo looked up, sniffed the delicately spiced aroma of fresh cilantro expertly blended with roasted Serrano peppers and asked, "How's my friend, Gus, today?"

"Gus says that you don't think the bond market has turned around yet. I do. Just look at housing starts and sales. They're finally falling. So is the Consumer

Confidence Index. I'm tellin' ya, my partner with the loose lips, this is what we've been waiting for. Economy looks like it's headed for a fall. I'm going long and strong into this bond bull market. By the way, Gus sent something over for you, too."

Neo smiled in anticipation. He sat quietly for a moment, pondering El's dilemma. "Have you ever heard of IDD—investment deficit disorder?"

"No. Such a thing doesn't exist."

Neo watched as El unwrapped his burrito. "I'm afraid it does." Greedo stopped the Mexican delicacy before it was halfway to his mouth. Neo continued, "Your symptoms are classic. You just can't wait to be the first to call the return to bond market prosperity and general economic calamity. You're itching to get in on the ground floor, to prove to everyone just how smart you are."

Greedo set down his as-yet-untasted lunch. "Yeah? So? I know the bond bull has arrived. I can feel his hot breath on my back."

"El, you *think* you know. You like the negative direction of housing and the apparent fall of the CCI. So do I. But I'm not betting the farm on them. Let's be rational here. We've come too far to blow it now."

Costly Starts and Flops

There will be many false starts and pullbacks throughout the bond market recovery that Greedo is counting on. Changing from bond market bear to bull or vice versa is a series of one step forward followed by two steps back. They never go all at once. Investors who jump in with everything they have are destined for a market smackdown and a wicked whipsaw.

ACTION STEP: AVOID BEING WHIPSAWED

The term comes from the push/pull action of lumberjacks cutting wood with a two-man saw—a whipsaw. Securities traders get whipsawed when a security price moves abruptly in one direction and then, soon after, it suddenly moves in exactly the opposite direction. Due to his acute case of IDD, El is in danger of jumping into the market just before it suddenly moves violently against him. His asset value will end up significantly below the price at which he originally bought it.

Avoid being whipsawed by waiting for the market to come to you. Do not overallocate to a market that has not yet proven itself.

Those with IDD, like El Greedo, see interest rates falling. They will buy long-term zero-coupon bonds and long-term bond funds. They want to lock in those higher yields before they disappear. They will also buy individual bonds on the longer end of the yield curve, thus extending their duration. They are certain that they have caught the coming bond bull market by the horns. They feel compelled to ride it up with longer durations. They believe that this aggressive strategy will maximize their profit.

The problem is that the market knows better. No one is bigger than the market. Not even El Greedo. The market is just waiting to smack down such naive investors and make them pay for their IDD. Table 9.1 is a report from the accompanying e-workbook that shows what we mean.

Notice that the movement in the portfolio's value whether interest rates move up or down isn't huge. After all, this particular portfolio is the nuclear winter portfolio, designed as a defensive strategy with short duration. It is indicative of a bond portfolio correctly positioned to survive a market that is going nowhere fast. However, imagine what would happen if, as El Greedo proposes, he extends their holdings further out on the yield curve—from the duration of 4.1 years in the nuclear winter portfolio to something closer to 9 years. He thinks they are taking advantage of a huge opportunity. However, if rates go against them—even for a short time—with a significantly longer duration, the value of their portfolio will plummet without mercy.

Investors afflicted with investment deficit disorder have little tolerance for seeing the value of their portfolios drop because of a trade they made. Their solution is to trade their way out of the loss. This usually creates even deeper losses. If they went the wrong way on the first trade, they're just as likely to go the wrong way on the next trade and the next. Such investors are not leading the pack, as Greedo intends on doing. Instead, they are just following the other lemmings, jumping off the cliff to their demise.

Strategy for Market Changes

Do not lose money by failing to follow your strategic plan. When it looks like the tide is turning, take a step—but just a step. Move some of your asset allocation into your green-shoot strategy at a measured pace. We'll show the green-shoot strategy in the next chapter.

Table 9.1 Portfolio Sensitivity: Nuclear Winter Bond Portfolios Only

Settlement Date	Face Value	Security	Coupon	Maturity	Purchase Price	Total Cost	Yield to Worst	Call Price	Δ in Value −150 bps	Δ in Value −100 bps	Δ in Value −50 bps	Δ in Value +50 bps	Δ in Value +100 bps	Δ in Value +150 bps
Corporate Bonds														
09/03/10	$125,000	Healthy Body Corp.	3.750%	03/15/12	101.000	$126,250	3.077%	100.000	$2,849	$1,890	$940	($931)	($1,853)	($2,765)
03/03/09	200,000	Gold Mining, Inc.	6.000%	02/15/13	98.000	196,000	6.227%	100.000	13,072	9,448	5,900	(978)	(4,312)	(7,577)
09/03/10	150,000	Big Blue	1.000%	03/15/13	99.900	149,850	1.040%	100.000	0	3,796	1,883	(1,855)	(3,683)	(5,484)
06/15/10	185,000	Lock N Load Arms Corp.	5.650%	01/15/14	98.750	182,688	6.041%	100.000	9,017	5,953	2,948	(2,892)	(5,728)	(8,511)
06/15/09	140,000	Operating Companies, Inc.	5.000%	01/15/14	96.000	134,400	5.737%	100.000	10,001	7,094	4,256	(1,221)	(3,863)	(6,443)
08/29/08	160,000	Oil Slick International	6.750%	01/25/14	95.000	152,000	7.645%	100.000	12,383	8,739	5,192	(1,621)	(4,894)	(8,080)
09/12/09	185,000	American Telecom	3.750%	02/15/14	98.000	181,300	4.007%	100.000	13,275	9,355	5,527	(1,864)	(5,431)	(8,915)
09/20/09	140,000	Laptop Computers Internat'l	5.780%	06/04/14	98.000	137,200	6.108%	100.000	9,662	6,682	3,773	(1,837)	(4,541)	(7,182)
09/03/10	200,000	Package Delivery International	3.800%	06/15/14	104.000	208,000	2.680%	100.000	11,328	7,473	3,698	(3,622)	(7,170)	(10,646)
10/01/07	190,000	AngelMed, Inc.	5.000%	09/13/14	91.000	172,900	5.814%	100.000	24,851	19,162	13,666	3,222	(1,738)	(6,532)

Date	Par Value	Description	Coupon	Maturity	Price	Face Value	Yield							
08/29/10	160,000	Drilling For You, Inc.	6.157%	02/15/15	96.000	153,600	7.221%	100.000	9,110	6,003	2,967	(2,900)	(5,733)	(8,503)
04/03/09	100,000	BioTech Logic, Inc.	4.750%	07/15/15	99.000	99,000	4.884%	100.000	8,667	5,780	2,983	(2,352)	(4,895)	(7,361)
09/03/10	300,000	Global Burgers Corp.	4.000%	09/03/15	107.000	321,000	2.502%	100.000	22,757	14,970	7,386	(7,193)	(14,200)	(21,025)
Subtotal Corp	$2,235,000					$2,214,188			$146,973	$106,345	$61,119	($26,043)	($68,041)	($109,024)
Municipal Bonds														
08/04/10	$210,000	Lower Colo Riv Auth. TEX	4.500%	05/15/14	102.010	$214,221	1.890%	100.000	$28,134	$23,896	$19,744	$11,696	$7,795	$3,973
08/04/10	170,000	Mobile Cnty Ala	4.500%	06/01/14	98.818	167,991	4.623%	100.000	10,384	7,285	4,250	(1,636)	(4,489)	(7,285)
09/04/10	100,000	Hawkeye State GO	1.250%	06/15/14	99.000	99,000	1.523%	100.000	5,636	3,718	1,839	(1,801)	(3,564)	(5,291)
09/04/10	100,000	Randolph County Water District	2.250%	10/31/14	102.000	102,000	1.749%	100.000	6,269	4,131	2,042	(1,996)	(3,947)	(5,855)
08/04/10	125,000	Evanston IL	4.000%	01/01/15	99.250	124,063	4.106%	100.000	8,148	5,506	2,925	(2,058)	(4,463)	(6,813)
09/04/10	300,000	Great State GO	1.750%	03/15/15	102.000	306,000	1.294%	100.000	0	13,644	6,737	(6,573)	(12,986)	(19,243)
08/04/10	50,000	Phoenix, AZ GO bond	2.250%	07/01/15	98.760	49,380	2.520%	100.000	3,557	2,340	1,155	(1,125)	(2,220)	(3,287)

(Continued)

Table 9.1 (Continued)

Settlement Date	Face Value	Security	Coupon	Maturity	Purchase Price	Total Cost	Yield to Worst	Call Price	Δ in Value −150 bps	Δ in Value −100 bps	Δ in Value −50 bps	Δ in Value +50 bps	Δ in Value +100 bps	Δ in Value +150 bps
08/04/10	50,000	KY Power Grid	3.875%	09/04/15	105.000	52,500	2.812%	100.000	3,781	2,487	1,227	(1,194)	(2,357)	(3,490)
09/04/10	330,000	Austin Sewer District	5.000%	09/15/15	110.000	363,000	0.991%	102.000	0	0	47,291	29,049	20,285	11,750
08/04/10	380,000	Shelby Cnty Tenn	4.750%	03/01/16	101.000	383,800	2.979%	100.000	62,476	51,516	40,869	20,474	10,708	1,217
08/04/10	300,000	Hays TEX Cons indpt. Sch. Dist	4.000%	08/15/16	108.000	324,000	0.988%	102.000	0	0	44,359	24,795	15,464	6,419
Subtotal Muni	$2,115,000					$2,185,954			$128,385	$114,521	$172,438	$69,632	$20,224	($27,904)
Total Bond Portfolio						$4,400,142			$275,358	$220,866	$233,557	$43,589	($47,817)	($136,928)

Begin with intermediate corporate bonds or their bond funds. Put no more than 10 to 15 percent of the portfolio into this strategy. The rest of the allocation sticks with the nuclear winter positions for now.

Doing this increases your portfolio's flexibility by starting to extend the duration. You don't have to be right on the market timing. At least the majority of your portfolio is rolling down the yield curve.

Without Neo's measured restraint, a trader like Greedo might switch suddenly to all long-term positions. He feels the need to take advantage of every last cent of the move he is convinced is coming. If he's wrong, he'll lose a substantial part of the portfolio. Going all in at this stage is like flooring the gas pedal in a school zone. No one in their right mind would do it. You may get lucky, but fate is against you.

Take a look at the price of the gold ETF (GLD) from 2005 through part of 2010 in Figure 9.1. Notice the sawtooth movements even in a raging bull market for gold.

Those with IDD would suffer significant losses on the down strokes—and there were several. We're not going to do that. We must gain more confidence

Figure 9.1   GLD Trends

Source: Bloomberg Finance LP. © 2010 Bloomberg Finance LP. All rights reserved. Used with permission.

and get verification that the bond indicators are right and the green shoots for the bond market are indeed sprouting. With more and more of our bond indicators pointing in a favorable direction (favorable for bonds, but on the downtrend for the general economy), we'll increase our stake in the green-shoot strategy to 20 percent. As the scenario unfolds and we're convinced the bond market is headed our way, then we'll slowly convert more of our portfolio into longer-duration positions. Along the way we'll begin deploying the 25 percent we had in cash during the nuclear winter.

That's how you avoid the siren song of investment deficit disorder. It is sometimes difficult to do. Especially when you want so much to believe that bond market prosperity is finally returning. Our advice is to remain detached and skeptical. It is better to miss out on some of the move than to be lured into a false start that costs you a material percentage of your portfolio.

If you're late to the party, the worst that happens is your profits are a little below what they might have been. If you are early to a party that never starts before it retreats, you'll suffer significant capital losses. We'll take fewer profits every time.

Coming up, Chapter 10, "Recognizing the Bond Market Green Shoots," shows you the signs to look for as the end of the bond market nuclear winter approaches, and the strategies to implement.

Chapter 10
RECOGNIZING THE BOND MARKET GREEN SHOOTS

Knowing how to recognize the green shoots of returning bond market prosperity is tricky. The yield curve changes; spreads begin narrowing; and the world of declining bond prices becomes a memory. These inflection points are what can either make you money or save you from losing money. Having the courage to act on this information—rebalancing your portfolio by reallocating assets, buying and selling bond positions—is what separates successful bond investors from the rest.

Earlier in this book we showed you how to stop the portfolio from hemorrhaging as the economy heated up and bonds entered a severe bear market. Then we showed you how to rebalance the portfolio to run at a safe level throughout the nuclear winter as the economy maintained its strength and continued to run hot. We kept our powder dry to fight another day.

That day has come—finally. Now it is time to identify the signs that the bond market is turning favorable and rebalance the portfolio accordingly. This is what we've been waiting for. It is the reason why we worked so hard to keep the portfolio intact. We're not talking mere survival, anymore. We're taking advantage of an extraordinary opportunity for profit.

When the green shoots of returning bond market prosperity appear, it is time to take an aggressive stand. Remember, a strong economy with inflation is death to bonds. Conversely, slow, non-inflationary growth is much more bond friendly.

The signs are obvious if you know where to look. Many investors see them. When they begin appearing, you will hear TV's talking heads touting some of them. However, most will urge caution. They are afraid of a false start only to be smacked down again by the bond gods.

We're not advocating doing something stupid that could unravel all the good decisions you've made to this point. Nevertheless, when the tea-leaves point to a decision, we make it. We don't wait. We aggressively—but prudently—follow a specific track designed to take advantage of unfolding opportunities. Our prepositioned milestones confirm that our course of action is correct. As we reach each milestone, we commit more capital to our strategy. As the bond market emerges from the most devastating nuclear winter in recent history, we position our portfolio to capitalize on opportunity. This is the way to make your money work harder for you than you could ever work for yourself. This is El Greedo's finest hour.

Telltale Trends

Keep your eye on the specific economic trends we introduced back in Chapter 1, "Warning Signs." They will tell you when the bond market green shoots have finally taken root. We don't think our favorite indicators will go in the same direction all at once. That would be too easy. Instead, we anticipate just some of them moving in the same positive direction (positive for the bond market is negative for the general economy).

At the end of the day, deciding when to begin rebalancing your portfolio out of the nuclear winter strategy and into bond prosperity will involve your own good judgment. Of course, unlike El Greedo, we take small steps, rebalancing small percentages of the overall portfolio until we're sure what we see isn't a sucker rally. As the green shoots take root we'll gain more and more confidence. As our conviction and confidence grows, we'll allocate increasingly larger percentages of the portfolio to the bond recovery strategy.

Like anything else associated with the bond market, we're skeptical. We wonder what can go wrong and how it will negatively impact our positions.

Indicators to Watch

We look at a number of indicators to tell us the bond market recovery is upon us. Most will see them as collateral damage to the economy:

- Unemployment rises.
- Housing starts and sales decline.
- Retail sales get sluggish.
- Durable goods sales decline.
- Auto sales decline.
- Travel expenditures decline.
- Fear of another recession looms.

These indicators serve to validate that the economy is softening. When this occurs, the bond market green shoots are ready to sprout. Taken together, these indicators paint a compelling picture that the economy is slowing. That is what bond investors are rooting for.

The risk is in acting prematurely. So what if you are a little late in rebalancing your portfolio to take advantage of bond market prosperity? The worst that happens is you don't make as large a profit as quickly as if you had caught the event right on the upswing—but you didn't lose anything, either. Rebalancing too much of your holdings out of the safe nuclear winter portfolio only to find the bond market smacked down again will unnecessarily lose you your principal. Like a skilled physician, first we *do no harm*.

Treasury Yields   It makes sense for Treasury yields to rise and bond prices to fall during an economic recovery. That is what caused the bond market nuclear winter. When the economy is doing well and is overheated, the Federal Reserve tightens its policies and interest rates rise. They often raise rates to a level that chokes off economic growth. This signals a turn for the better in Bondland.

How can you tell? Watch the yield curve. The strongest bond market rallies occur during an inverted yield curve (short-term rates are higher than long-term rates).

Our suggestion is to also observe movement in Treasury yields. Don't make any rebalancing decisions from this (or any single) indicator alone. Instead, use it to add to several other indicators to form a consensus opinion on economic direction. We're looking for indications that the overheated economy is cooling and headed downward. That will help us refine our bond market timing to incrementally take positions with longer duration bonds.

Improvement in Municipal Credit   During the nuclear winter, municipalities had all sorts of credit problems. Many municipal bond issuers had badly unbalanced budgets. Their financial ratios were out of whack. During 2009 and 2010, a goodly number of municipalities found access to the public debt markets easy because demand for municipal bonds was great. Then came the nuclear winter. This thrust many issuers to the verge of default. Even a robust economy was insufficient to fix all the unfunded liabilities that had built up over the years.

One of the bond market green shoots will be the municipal bond issuer's awakening that they must get their financial houses in order. This will require elected officials to make decisions unpopular to the special interests so vital in sweeping them into office and keeping them there. These same officials will have to place the greater public good over their own reelection.

Frankly, we don't see this happening. Too many of our elected officeholders are skilled in little else but winning political campaigns. Their concept of success does not include moving our country forward. Instead, many focus solely on getting and retaining their offices.

Corporate Bonds   As we saw in the Great Recession of 2008–2009, corporations became very prudent. CEOs created cease-and-desist orders for their companies. They ceased and desisted from squandering precious cash on share repurchases and acquisitions. Cash became a valued asset once again. Debt repayment (*deleveraging*, to some) was suddenly a legitimate corporate goal.

The same will happen as we exit the bond bear market and the nuclear winter. Fiscal and financial prudence will lead the way into the green-shoot phase. That is exactly when bond investors should extend duration. Go for the gusto. Lock-and-load portfolios with yield.

How do you follow this trend? Read all the financial publications: *Wall Street Journal, Barron's, Forbes, Fortune,* and Bloomberg.com.

The Green-Shoots Rebalancing Strategy

Remember that the green-shoots phase refers to the prosperity of your bond portfolio and a *weaker* economy. As the economy declines, bonds become more attractive. Continue to look for the indicators that confirm the economy is cooling off and losing steam. Maybe you haven't seen all indicators point to higher bond prices and lower yields. But you can see enough that are showing a positive trend for bonds to convince you the time has come to start rebalancing the portfolio out of the bond nuclear winter and into the prosperity strategy.

Rebalancing now simply becomes a matter of timing, allocation, and knowing which positions to sell and what to replace them with. An overheated economy, mixed with inflation, then stirred by the Federal Reserve's tight monetary policy will eventually cause a decline in interest rates and a resurgence in the attractiveness of bonds. The bond market's green shoots will sprout only when a strong or overheated economy cools. If a spike in interest rates occurs due to other forces, then bond prices will just as easily get nuked.

During 2010, we had the most accommodative Federal Reserve policies ever imagined. The gold, commodity, and currency markets were all saying the United States was printing too much money out of thin air. Eventually, this will be inflationary. On top of that, the U.S. economy was saddled with huge debt. As a result, the bond market green shoots may lay dormant for longer than we anticipate. When the new bond prosperity does occur, you need to know how to rebalance your bond portfolio to take maximum advantage of the tremendous opportunity presented you. Chapter 11, "Rebalancing into Bond Market Prosperity," shows you how.

REBALANCING INTO BOND MARKET PROSPERITY

Day 377: Sunny's Hand Car Wash, 3:45 P.M.

Neo watched the four guys with hand-mops soap up his brother-in-law's Kia. Downsizing from the BMW had badly injured Greedo's ego. He flipped the page of his latest copy of *Marilyn Cohen's Bond Smart Investor* newsletter.

"How much longer you think our winter of discontent is gonna last?" asked Greedo.

Neo had finally reached his conclusion: This was the time to rebalance into the green-shoot strategy. He reverently set the invaluable newsletter on his lap. "Glad you asked, my astutely intuitive partner. I think the time has come to begin rebalancing the portfolio."

Greedo paused for a minute, considering the weight of Neo's words. He watched the guys spray-rinse the little Kia. Soap streamed off the slab-sided doors of the pea-soup-colored car. This was the news he had waited for throughout the past 13 months. "How so?" he asked, hoping his trading partner could convince him.

"Indicators say so," began Neo. "I've looked at the employment numbers. I've read the minutes of the last three Fed meetings. I've watched the bond vigilantes lose their momentum—"

"Where do you get all this stuff?"

Neo picked up the *Marilyn Cohen's Bond Smart Investor* from the bench. "Right here," he waved the green-bannered 15 pages of bond market intelligence before El. "Takes about 20 minutes a month to read. I always keep it at my desk and refer to it constantly when we're figuring out our trading strategy."

"So what do we do?"

Sunny walked by and said to Neo, "Hey, partner. You see this issue yet?" He waved his copy of the green-bannered newsletter at Neo. "Looks like our time has come my friend. Maybe finally you get your bro-in-law out of that little Kia, eh?"

"Just what I was thinking, Sunny," said Neo. To Greedo he explained, "We'll figure out the first 10 percent of the portfolio to rebalance."

Greedo called out, "Hey, Sunny. Tell me, why do you work at a car wash?"

The hardworking man set down a pile of blue towels and said, "Mr. Greedo, you think this is all I do? I have four more car washes. Each grosses $2 million a year. I also have an interest in a gym, a chain of Mexican restaurants, some dry cleaners, and apartment houses. Then there is the trailer park on the beach. Love the cash flow from our 500 trailer pads. You ask why? I'll tell you. If I didn't have my car wash, who would wash the ugly pea-green Kia, Mr. Greedo?" He picked up the towels and walked away, laughing.

Changing Portfolio Strategies

Remember, a strengthening bond market usually happens in a weakening economy. Shifting from the nuclear winter strategy to one designed to take advantage of oncoming bond market prosperity isn't rocket science, but it is economically counterintuitive. As Neo said, you watch the indicators. When they begin to point in the same direction, you pay attention. When several months go by and they're still telling you the time has come, you begin to move into the *green-shoots strategy*.

Overview of the Green-Shoots Rebalancing

We, like most professional money managers, have an order of priorities for rebalancing new accounts that come to us. These are usually loaded with funds, individual positions, and cash. To rebalance the portfolio from the nuclear winter to one that will profit as the economy slows, first determine how much cash you have to work with.

The green-shoots strategy is one that is fully invested and without much excess cash. The logic is that the positions we've selected will pay more than any money market account. The only money left on the bench is that which you will need to live and to have as an emergency cushion. The rest goes into the portfolio.

Sift through all individual bond issues currently in the portfolio. Study their balance sheets, debt distribution, and material events for munis. For corporate bonds, look up their earnings history. Prioritize which positions to begin peeling off. Know what you'll replace them with so the transition is seamless and there is no time where idle cash sits around not working.

Keep repeating this procedure until you've sold all the bonds and bond funds that no longer fit the green-shoots strategy and the proceeds are redeployed to positions consistent with the newly prospering bond market.

Types of Securities and Speed of Implementation   The purpose of this new rebalancing is to take advantage of the profit-making opportunities found in a recovering bond market. The types of positions include:

- Corporate bonds
- Municipal bonds
- Bond funds
- Other types of securities

How fast should we implement the rebalance strategy? The answer may sound cryptic: just as fast as the market tells you to. This means that you should implement your new investment strategy in increments as you gain confidence that the green shoots have indeed taken hold. The increments we recommend are:

- 10 percent
- 25 percent
- 50 percent
- 75 percent
- 100 percent

We don't add the next increment until we see further evidence that the economy is indeed cooling down. For example, say we've already rebalanced the first 10 percent of the portfolio and we're looking to rebalance the next 15 percent to give us a total of 25 percent in the green-shoots strategy. When do we pull the trigger on that next 15 percent? It could be when a series of indicators move in our direction for the third straight month. Let's say we watch six indicators for this favorable trend:

1. Employment rates
2. Consumer confidence index
3. Home foreclosure rates
4. Housing starts and sales
5. Retail sales
6. Interest rates

If all six are moving toward bond market prosperity (a general economic downturn) for three straight months, we might take the next step and rebalance that next 15 percent of the portfolio. The move from the now-25 percent to 50 percent, then 75 percent, and finally 100 percent rebalanced works the same way. Don't get antsy and move too quickly. Remain skeptical that the new bond prosperity is for real. Make the economy convince you that it has turned downward and won't rebound before rebalancing the next tranche.

Changing the Duration Strategy   A significant part of the change from a nuclear winter to a bond market prosperity configuration concerns duration. Look at the report in Table 11.1 before rebalancing into prosperity.

Table 11.1 Portfolio Appraisal With Yield to Worst: Nuclear Winter—All Portfolios

Settlement Date	Face Value	Security	Coupon	Maturity	Purchase Price	Total Cost	% of Assets	Yield to Maturity	Yield to Worst	Modified Duration
Corporate Bonds										
09/03/10	$125,000	Healthy Body Corp.	3.750%	03/15/12	101.000	$126,250	1%	3.077%	3.077%	1.457
03/03/09	200,000	Gold Mining, Inc.	6.000%	02/15/13	98.000	196,000	2%	6.582%	6.227%	3.447
09/03/10	150,000	Big Blue	1.000%	03/15/13	99.900	149,850	2%	1.040%	1.040%	2.483
06/15/10	185,000	Lock N Load Arms Corp.	5.650%	01/15/14	98.750	182,688	2%	6.041%	6.041%	3.122
06/15/09	140,000	Operating Companies, Inc.	5.000%	01/15/14	96.000	134,400	2%	6.010%	5.737%	3.937
08/29/08	160,000	Oil Slick International	6.750%	01/25/14	95.000	152,000	2%	7.902%	7.645%	4.391
09/12/09	185,000	American Telecom	3.750%	02/15/14	98.000	181,300	2%	4.250%	4.007%	4.018
09/20/09	140,000	Laptop Computers International	5.780%	06/04/14	98.000	137,200	2%	6.275%	6.108%	3.986
09/03/10	200,000	Package Delivery International	3.800%	06/15/14	104.000	208,000	2%	2.680%	2.680%	3.491
10/01/07	190,000	AngelMed, Inc.	5.000%	09/13/14	91.000	172,900	2%	6.637%	5.814%	5.693
08/29/10	160,000	Drilling For You, Inc.	6.157%	02/15/15	96.000	153,600	2%	7.221%	7.221%	3.809
04/03/09	100,000	BioTech Logic, Inc.	4.750%	07/15/15	99.000	99,000	1%	4.936%	4.884%	5.315
09/03/10	300,000	Global Burgers Corp.	4.000%	09/03/15	107.000	321,000	4%	2.502%	2.502%	4.541
Subtotal Corp	$2,235,000					$2,214,188	25%			
Municipal Bonds										
08/04/10	$210,000	Lower Colo Riv Auth. TEX	4.500%	05/15/14	102.010	$214,221	2%	3.921%	1.890%	3.422
08/04/10	170,000	Mobile Cnty Ala	4.500%	06/01/14	98.818	167,991	2%	4.840%	4.623%	3.445
09/04/10	100,000	Hawkeye State GO	1.250%	06/15/14	104.000	104,000	1%	0.188%	0.188%	3.693

(Continued)

Table 11.1 (Continued)

Settlement Date	Face Value	Security	Coupon	Maturity	Purchase Price	Total Cost	% of Assets	Yield to Maturity	Yield to Worst	Modified Duration
09/04/10	100,000	Randolph County Water District	2.250%	10/31/14	102.000	102,000	1%	1.749%	1.749%	3.929
08/04/10	125,000	Evanston IL	4.000%	01/01/15	99.250	124,063	1%	4.187%	4.106%	3.986
09/04/10	300,000	Great State GO	1.750%	03/15/15	102.000	306,000	3%	1.294%	1.294%	4.314
08/04/10	50,000	Phoenix, AZ GO bond	4.750%	07/01/15	98.760	49,380	1%	5.037%	4.994%	4.305
08/04/10	50,000	KY Power Grid	1.875%	09/04/15	105.000	52,500	1%	0.867%	0.867%	4.822
09/04/10	330,000	Austin Sewer District	1.875%	09/15/15	103.000	339,900	4%	1.258%	1.258%	4.757
08/04/10	380,000	Shelby Cnty Tenn	4.750%	03/01/16	101.000	383,800	4%	4.544%	2.979%	4.762
08/04/10	300,000	Hays TEX Cons indpt. Sch. Dist	4.000%	08/15/16	99.240	297,720	3%	4.143%	4.112%	5.207
08/31/10	100,000	Las Vegas Monorail	5.625%	01/01/32	27.250	27,250	0%	21.377%	21.377%	4.976
Subtotal Muni	$2,215,000					$2,168,824	25%			
Subtotal bond portfolio only						$4,383,012	50%			
Average Weighted Yields for bond portfolio only								4.046%	3.714%	
Average Weighted Duration for bond portfolio only										4.121

Other Securities

10/12/10	$2,175,000	Schwab Money Market Fund	N/A	N/A	100.000	$2,175,000	25%	N/A	N/A	N/A
10/12/10	300,000	Black Rock Global Floating Rate Income Trust	N/A	N/A	100.000	300,000	3%	N/A	N/A	N/A
10/12/10	200,000	iShares Municipal Series	N/A	N/A	100.000	200,000	2%	N/A	N/A	N/A
10/12/10	200,000	Claymore Bullet Shares Corporate Bond ETF	N/A	N/A	100.000	200,000	2%	N/A	N/A	N/A
10/12/10	300,000	Fidelity Floating Rate High Income Fund	N/A	N/A	100.000	300,000	3%	N/A	N/A	N/A
10/12/10	200,000	Sallie Mae CMTs	N/A	N/A	100.000	200,000	2%	N/A	N/A	N/A
10/12/10	300,000	Oppenhiemer Senior Floating Rate	N/A	N/A	100.000	300,000	3%	N/A	N/A	N/A
10/12/10	300,000	ProShares Ultra Short 7-10 Year ETF	N/A	N/A	100.000	300,000	3%	N/A	N/A	N/A
10/12/10	400,000	LEAPS	N/A	N/A	100.000	400,000	5%	N/A	N/A	N/A
Subtotal Other Securities	$4,375,000					$4,375,000	50%			
Total Portfolio						$8,758,012	100.0%			

Note that the duration before we rebalance into the prosperity strategy is just 4.1 (lower-right corner in the grayed box). This is just what we had wanted during the nuclear winter. It was safe, no matter what interest rates did—especially if they rose, which we anticipate throughout the nuclear winter.

However, as the U.S. economy weakens, interest rates will fall. This is advantageous to bond investors. So why would we not want to participate in the rising prices of our bonds? Of course we would. The way we do this is to extend the maturities of our bond portfolio farther out onto the yield curve. We buy bonds with longer maturities. This increases the duration of the portfolio. Our target duration for the green-shoots scenario is from seven to nine years. Quite a change from the safety of the nuclear winter's four-year duration.

For some of the positions where we like the issuer—we've reviewed their balance sheets and analyst reports; we've decided this is an issuer we'll stick with—this may just require swapping out the short-maturity bond we already own for one with a longer maturity. For others, we may trade a current position for a completely new issuer with a longer maturity.

Asset Allocation Strategy

We put our money where it will do us the most good. We believe that an economic environment of slower growth should strongly favor corporate bonds. We must carefully select the corporate issuers. We want companies whose business models run countercyclical to the economic trend, as we did with the nuclear winter strategy.

Corporate Bonds   Generally, we'll allocate a significant majority of our assets to corporations with substantial cash. We want to own bonds issued by companies that didn't make crazy acquisitions that were funded by debt. We'll want fortress balance sheets that can withstand a less robust economic environment.

Municipal Bonds   Conversely, we won't allocate much of the portfolio to municipal bonds. We don't believe the state, county, city, and district governments will make much progress toward cleaning up the mess their elected officials created. The municipal bonds we will hold are a safety net for our portfolio. Some will be prerefunded and escrowed to maturity. The munis we hold will be for essential services. Some will be double-barrel bonds with secondary payment sources in the event that the primary source fails. Don't expect any capital appreciation on the municipal bonds in this portfolio. We buy them for the yield we receive.

Bond Funds   During the bond market's nuclear winter we did not hold any bond funds. We got out of them before the market tanked. However, things have changed. As the economy slows, bond funds can add a nice performance enhancement to the portfolio. Further, they are easy to buy and provide a good diversification. We'll allocate a minor portion of the portfolio to selected bond funds.

Cash   As we rebalance the portfolio toward the green-shoots strategy, we'll spend most all of the cash we have. We want to be fully invested to take maximum advantage of the improving bond market. The only reason we see for leaving cash on the sidelines is to keep some available for day-to-day living expenses and in case of emergency. Otherwise, cash should be fully deployed.

Another point on cash: As the economy slides and the bond market improves, idle cash becomes an expensive, wasting asset. Every day that cash sits on the bench in a money market account incurs an opportunity cost. The more the bond market improves, the higher the opportunity cost. When a bond matures or when a coupon comes due you should have a preplanned place for it to go *before* you receive it.

Look at Table 11.2. We lifted it straight from the automated e-workbook that accompanies this book. It shows all the scheduled interest income and principal maturities for the entire bond portfolio configured for the nuclear winter before we rebalanced it into prosperity. If you manually kept tabs on just when your bonds pay their interest or when they would mature and repay your principal, now you can toss away your pencils. You have a better, more accurate tool right here in this convenient report shown by month and year. **The e-workbook comes free with your purchase of this book. The appendix shows you where to log onto the Internet and how to download it right to your computer.**

Table 11.2 Monthly Cash Flows Nuclear Winter—All Portfolios

Interest Income

	2010	2011	2012	2013	2014	2015	2016	2017	2018	2019	2020
January	$0	$19,564	$19,564	$19,564	$19,564	$5,438	$0	$0	$0	$0	$0
February	0	20,394	20,394	20,394	14,394	10,926	6,000	0	0	0	0
March	0	34,713	34,713	32,369	31,619	26,869	9,025	0	0	0	0
April	0	0	0	0	0	0	0	0	0	0	0
May	0	5,850	5,850	5,850	5,850	0	0	0	0	0	0
June	0	12,296	12,296	12,296	12,296	0	0	0	0	0	0
July	0	19,564	19,564	19,564	5,438	2,938	0	0	0	0	0
August	0	20,394	20,394	14,394	10,926	6,000	-6,000	0	0	0	0
September	0	34,713	32,369	31,619	31,619	24,244	0	0	0	0	0
October	0	0	0	0	1,125	0	0	0	0	0	0
November	4,725	5,850	5,850	5,850	0	0	0	0	0	0	0
December	12,296	12,296	12,296	12,296	0	0	0	0	0	0	0
Total	$17,021	$185,633	$183,289	$174,196	$132,830	$76,413	$21,025	$0	$0	$0	$0

Principal Paydowns

	2010	2011	2012	2013	2014	2015	2016	2017	2018	2019	2020
January	$0	$0	$0	$0	$485,000	$125,000	$0	$0	$0	$0	$0
February	0	0	0	200,000	185,000	160,000	0	0	0	0	0
March	0	0	125,000	150,000	0	300,000	380,000	0	0	0	0
April	0	0	0	0	0	0	0	0	0	0	0
May	0	0	0	0	210,000	0	0	0	0	0	0

	2010	2011	2012	2013	2014	2015	2016	2017	2018	2019	2020
June	0	0	0	0	610,000	0	0	0	0	0	0
July	0	0	0	0	0	150,000	0	0	0	0	0
August	0	0	0	0	0	0	300,000	0	0	0	0
September	0	0	0	0	190,000	680,000	0	0	0	0	0
October	0	2,175,000	0	0	600,000	700,000	300,000	300,000	400,000	0	0
November	0	0	0	0	0	0	0	0	0	0	0
December	0	0	0	0	0	0	0	0	0	0	0
Total	$0	$2,175,000	$125,000	$350,000	$2,280,000	$2,115,000	$980,000	$300,000	$400,000	$0	$0

Total Cashflows

	2010	2011	2012	2013	2014	2015	2016	2017	2018	2019	2020
January	0	19,564	19,564	19,564	504,564	130,438	0	0	0	0	0
February	0	20,394	20,394	220,394	199,394	170,926	6,000	0	0	0	0
March	0	34,713	159,713	182,369	31,619	326,869	389,025	0	0	0	0
April	0	0	0	0	0	0	0	0	0	0	0
May	0	5,850	5,850	5,850	215,850	0	0	0	0	0	0
June	0	12,296	12,296	12,296	622,296	0	0	0	0	0	0
July	0	19,564	19,564	19,564	5,438	152,938	0	0	0	0	0
August	0	20,394	20,394	14,394	10,926	6,000	306,000	0	0	0	0
September	0	34,713	32,369	31,619	221,619	704,244	0	0	0	0	0
October	0	2,175,000	0	0	601,125	700,000	300,000	300,000	400,000	0	0
November	4,725	5,850	5,850	5,850	0	0	0	0	0	0	0
December	12,296	12,296	12,296	12,296	0	0	0	0	0	0	0
Total	17,021	2,360,633	308,289	524,196	2,412,830	2,191,413	1,001,025	300,000	400,000	0	0

Summary of the Asset Allocation Strategy

Here are the asset allocation percentages we suggest for the bond market green-shoots strategy:

- Corporates: 70 percent
- Munis: 20 percent
- Governments and bond funds: 10 percent
- Cash: 0 percent

Corporate Bond Strategy

We have three objectives in rebalancing the corporate bond portfolio:

1. Increase the asset allocation to 70 percent of the entire portfolio.
2. Increase the duration to an average of from seven to nine years.
3. Rebalance into corporate bond issuers that will leverage the slowing economy in their favor.

This isn't an easy task. It requires research and the ability to get out of the positions that have served you well throughout the nuclear winter but are no longer appropriate when the bond market returns to prosperity. It is necessary to change horses. Those nuclear winter corporate bonds may not maximize your portfolio's potential as we head into an era of bond market affluence.

Which Corporates to Buy

Let's begin by identifying the sectors most likely to do well as the economy loses its lift and once again sags. We want sectors that prosper in a soft economy. These include:

- Pharmaceuticals
- Oil and gas
- Big-box retailers
- Fast-food restaurants
- Do-it-yourself automobile parts and fix-it stores

- Discount stores
- Home entertainment providers
- Utilities

These are the sectors we'll use to populate the corporate bond section of the portfolio. As always, we won't overcommit to any single name. Make a rule that no single position accounts for more than 3 to 5 percent of the entire portfolio. Be sure to include in that percentage the holdings of any bond funds appearing elsewhere in the portfolio.

Additionally, restrict your corporate holdings to large and medium-sized, stable companies. They should have substantial amounts of cash and manageable debt structures. Their manufacturing infrastructure (plants, mills, and other production facilities) should already be in place. Few companies will commit to large capital investment programs in a lagging economy. Essentially, choose those companies that are mature and with proven management.

Sectors to Avoid

As the bond market enters the green-shoots stage and the economy weakens, avoid leveraged companies. Buy names that will prosper when economic growth slows and consumers trade down-market for goods and services.

As for the financials, what can we say? They have disappointed so many investors. It seems that every month a new disaster befalls the sector. We don't have any financials in the green-shoots corporate bond portfolio in Table 11.3.

Note that we've made some significant changes from the corporate positions we had during the nuclear winter. First, see how we've stretched out the duration by moving into longer maturities. Duration is now between seven and nine years. This allows the portfolio to appreciate in value as interest rates fall and bond prices rise.

Next, we added about $4 million to the corporate bond portfolio. This is what rebalancing is all about. We redeploy our assets to the places where they will do us the most good. During the new bond market prosperity, that place is definitely in corporate bonds. Finally, we stuck to the rule of avoiding any undue concentration by limiting each position to a maximum of 5 percent of the entire portfolio.

Table 11.3 Portfolio Appraisal With Yield to Worst: Green Shoots Strategy Corporate Bonds—All Portfolios

Settlement Date	Face Value	Security	Coupon	Maturity	Purchase Price	Total Cost	% of Assets	Yield to Maturity	Yield to Worst	Modified Duration
Corporate Bonds										
09/03/10	$400,000	Pharmacom International	5.800%	06/15/21	102.000	$408,000	5%	5.550%	5.208%	7.879
01/19/11	430,000	Blue Sky Computers	5.000%	03/15/22	99.940	429,742	5%	5.006%	5.006%	8.329
01/04/11	430,000	Auto Center Stores	5.450%	10/20/22	101.000	434,300	5%	5.334%	5.317%	8.546
01/14/11	214,000	Oregon Pharmaceutical Corp.	4.670%	12/20/22	96.000	205,440	2%	5.122%	5.122%	8.959
01/12/11	400,000	Oil Slick International	6.750%	01/25/23	91.000	364,000	4%	7.923%	7.923%	7.655
01/12/11	400,000	American Telecom	4.750%	02/15/23	99.000	396,000	5%	4.860%	4.860%	8.924
09/20/09	430,000	Laptop Computers Internat'l	5.780%	06/04/23	91.000	391,300	4%	6.798%	6.798%	8.953
01/15/11	400,000	Southern Power Grid	6.750%	07/20/23	96.000	384,000	4%	7.241%	7.241%	7.981
01/12/11	400,000	Global Burgers Corp.	5.700%	10/20/23	97.000	388,000	4%	6.039%	6.039%	8.796
01/11/11	400,000	AngelMed, Inc.	5.000%	09/13/24	95.000	380,000	4%	5.525%	5.500%	9.526
01/15/11	400,000	Deep Discount Retail Stores Federation	6.120%	10/20/24	93.000	372,000	4%	6.915%	6.915%	8.872
01/12/11	430,000	Residential Entertainment Systems, Inc.	7.500%	11/20/24	98.000	421,400	5%	7.736%	7.736%	8.375
01/15/11	430,000	Operating Companies, Inc.	5.000%	01/15/25	93.000	399,900	5%	5.734%	5.734%	9.791
01/13/11	430,000	Federal Appliance Restoratoin	5.800%	04/21/25	98.000	421,400	5%	6.010%	6.010%	9.435
01/07/11	430,000	Big Blue Box	5.900%	08/20/25	101.000	434,300	5%	5.797%	5.750%	9.526
01/10/11	320,000	Wheels Corp.	7.800%	10/20/25	91.000	291,200	3%	8.904%	8.904%	8.205
Subtotal Corp	$6,344,000					$6,120,982	70%			

Municipal Bond Strategy

We'll allocate about 20 percent of total assets to the green-shoots municipal bond portfolio. The tricky part is knowing what bonds to populate this 20 percent with. As always, leg into the full allocation gradually, going only as fast as the market convinces you to go.

Sectors

The municipal bond sectors we recommend—even for the green-shoots strategy—are for safety. Knowing the self-serving agenda of so many elected leaders and their general naïveté in fiscal matters, we recommend sticking with those sectors having the highest probability of performing. These include:

- General obligation bonds (GOs)
- Essential services
- School bonds
- Bonds with state aid, such as the school intercept bonds
- Airport revenue bonds
- Water and sewer bonds

These sectors either have the full taxing authority of the issuer—such as the GOs—to make good any shortfall or some other safety net. In the case of the state aid bonds, there is a secondary payment source. For the state intercept bonds, should the municipal issuer fall on hard times, a trustee steps in and physically intercepts tax payments made to the issuer and disburses them to bond holders. Essential-service bonds—water and sewer—and revenue bonds with a reliable source of revenue for payment purposes—airport bonds—are also a good bet.

We certainly don't want bonds whose payment source is discretionary. Toll-road bonds are such an animal. The toll road in question may suddenly no longer be advantageous to commuters and could fall out of favor. The forecast usage could be way off, making repayment of the bonds impossible.

Tax anticipation bonds are another sector investors should avoid. These are bonds issued by entities that can incur cash flow problems. Investors should shun issuers whose fiscal house is in such disarray that they can't wait for the normal timing of cash receipts.

States Providing a Safe Haven Within the various bond sectors, there are a number of fiscally responsible states to favor over the others (as of 2010, at least). These include:

- Texas
- Tennessee
- Virginia
- Utah
- Minnesota
- Indiana
- North and South Carolina
- Arkansas
- Maryland
- Wisconsin

The percentage of the municipal bond portfolio allocated to each of these is a judgment call depending on your state of residence. The tax benefits of your home state may compensate you for the added risk not only of investing in your own state but in any undue concentration you may knowingly undertake. Generally, prudent investors stay as diversified as possible in their municipal bond portfolios. Don't put a majority of your municipal bond allocation in a single issue, district, city, or county. Spread it around. Certainly, don't put any more than 5 percent of the total portfolio into any one municipal bond issue unless it is prerefunded or escrowed to maturity with State and Local Government Series (SLGS).

Duration in the Muni Portfolio

Just as we did with corporates, extend the maturities of the municipal bond issues into which you are rebalancing. This allows you to take advantage of the decline in interest rates.

For the regular municipal bonds, extend your maturities out nine or ten years. For the zero-coupon munis you buy, go out 15 to 20 years. This effectively locks in the high yields at the top, just when the green shoots are beginning to sprout.

Table 11.4 shows the rebalanced municipal bond portfolio configured to take advantage of the new bond market prosperity. Note that it comprises 20 percent of the entire portfolio, durations for each position range from seven to nine years, and no position accounts for more than 5 percent of the portfolio.

Government Bond Strategy

A small part of the green-shoots bond portfolio should include some governments. They provide additional safety and stability. The list of government agencies to populate your green-shoots portfolio is a short one. We want a guaranteed payment from the U.S. government. The only two agencies that provide this iron-clad guarantee are:

- Federal Farm Credit
- Federal Home Loan Bank

For these, we recommend a slightly shorter duration of from five to six years.

We also want a small position in Treasurys. However, we use the 30-year Treasurys as a trading vehicle rather than as a buy-and-hold core position. We recommend doing this using ETFs. This temporary holding facility provides a good yield, safety, and liquidity. Buy the longest duration treasury ETF available.

Bond Fund Strategy

During the nuclear winter, investors who refuse to leave their bond funds will get hosed. As interest rates rise, the value of these funds will plummet. There will be a mass exodus. Fund managers won't be able to stop the cash hemorrhage. Some may fold. Redemption risk is real.

Still, bond funds are a legitimate investment category in the green-shoots environment. After all, for many investors, researching, buying, and holding individual bonds is too much work.

The strategy for rebalancing some of the unallocated cash into bond funds should focus on large, domestic investment-grade and high-yield bond funds.

Table 11.4 Portfolio Appraisal With Yield to Worst: Green Shoot Municipal Bond Holdings

Settlement Date	Face Value	Security	Coupon	Maturity	Purchase Price	Total Cost	% of Assets	Yield to Maturity	Yield to Worst	Modified Duration
Municipal Bonds										
01/23/11	$100,000	Charleston SC Airport	0.000%	04/15/20	65.000	$65,000	1%	4.723%	2.253%	9.015
08/04/10	300,000	Hays TX Cons Indpt. Sch. Dist	4.000%	08/15/20	99.240	297,720	3%	4.093%	4.093%	8.033
08/04/10	50,000	Maryland Power Grid	4.875%	09/04/20	110.000	55,000	1%	3.679%	2.753%	7.901
09/04/10	300,000	Great State of TX GO	3.750%	03/15/21	104.500	313,500	4%	3.242%	3.027%	8.557
09/04/10	330,000	Austin Sewer District	3.875%	09/15/21	107.500	354,750	4%	3.068%	2.288%	8.874
09/04/10	100,000	Randolph County Water District	4.250%	10/31/21	108.000	108,000	1%	3.383%	3.383%	8.826
08/04/10	380,000	Shelby Cnty Tenn	4.750%	03/01/22	101.000	383,800	4%	4.637%	4.637%	8.673
02/10/11	100,000	Wisconsin State GO	4.750%	08/15/22	95.000	95,000	1%	5.337%	5.337%	8.484
02/03/11	50,000	Indiana Public Building Bonds	4.500%	12/15/22	98.000	49,000	1%	4.722%	4.688%	9.024
02/14/11	72,000	MN State Edutcation Fund	4.500%	09/15/23	85.000	61,200	1%	6.237%	6.237%	8.977
Subtotal Muni	$1,782,000					$1,782,970	20%			

Portfolio Reports

Day 412: War Room, 1:25 P.M.

Neo stood up in front of his computer and stretched his arms overhead.

"That it?" asked Greedo, reluctantly setting aside his copy of *Marilyn Cohen's Bond Smart Investor.* He was now a true believer in the newsletter.

"Done, done, and done. The green shoots of bond market prosperity are upon us. We have completely rebalanced the portfolio. I see you're a reader now," said Neo indicating the green-bannered newsletter.

"Yeah. I'm into the second month of my free trial subscription."

"Are you going to subscribe?"

Greedo looked at his sister's husband, "You kidding? I already did. Used the web site and passwords on the second-to-last page of this book. Best advice you ever gave me. Say, is all cash deployed?"

"Yes, my skeptical relative. Corporates account for 70 percent; municipal bonds, for 20 percent; the rest is in bond funds, Treasurys, government agencies—"

"But just two agencies, right?"

"Exactly, Elvin. Federal Home Loan Bank and Federal Farm Credit Bank."

Green-Shoots Portfolio

We've described the individual pieces of the green-shoots portfolio. It is now time to show what the entire portfolio looks like. Greedo and Neo did exactly what they said they would do—rebalance into a configuration intended to take maximum advantage of an economic downturn and return to prosperity for the bond market. We took all the reports shown in the following tables from the automated e-workbook that was free with the purchase of this book. You can access the free download using directions found in the appendix of this book.

Portfolio Appraisal Report

Table 11.5 shows the entire rebalanced portfolio:

Table 11.5 Portfolio Appraisal With Yield to Worst: Green Shoots Strategy—All Portfolios

Settlement Date	Face Value	Security	Coupon	Maturity	Purchase Price	Total Cost	% of Assets	Yield to Maturity	Yield to Worst	Modified Duration
Corporate Bonds										
09/03/10	$400,000	Pharmacom International	5.800%	06/15/21	102.000	$408,000	5%	5.550%	5.208%	7.879
01/19/11	430,000	Blue Sky Computers	5.000%	03/15/22	99.940	429,742	5%	5.006%	5.006%	8.329
01/04/11	430,000	Auto Center Stores	5.450%	10/20/22	101.000	434,300	5%	5.334%	5.317%	8.546
01/14/11	214,000	Oregon Pharmaceutical Corp.	4.670%	12/20/22	96.000	205,440	2%	5.122%	5.122%	8.959
01/12/11	400,000	Oil Slick International	6.750%	01/25/23	91.000	364,000	4%	7.923%	7.923%	7.655
01/12/11	400,000	American Telecom	4.750%	02/15/23	99.000	396,000	5%	4.860%	4.860%	8.924
09/20/09	430,000	Laptop Computers International	5.780%	06/04/23	91.000	391,300	4%	6.798%	6.798%	8.953
01/15/11	400,000	Southern Power Grid	6.750%	07/20/23	96.000	384,000	4%	7.241%	7.241%	7.981
01/12/11	400,000	Global Burgers Corp.	5.700%	10/20/23	97.000	388,000	4%	6.039%	6.039%	8.796
01/11/11	400,000	AngelMed, Inc.	5.000%	09/13/24	95.000	380,000	4%	5.525%	5.500%	9.526
01/15/11	400,000	Deep Discount Retail Stores Federation	6.120%	10/20/24	93.000	372,000	4%	6.915%	6.915%	8.872
01/12/11	430,000	Residential Entertainment Systems, Inc.	7.500%	11/20/24	98.000	421,400	5%	7.736%	7.736%	8.375
01/15/11	430,000	Operating Companies, Inc.	5.000%	01/15/25	93.000	399,900	5%	5.734%	5.734%	9.791
01/13/11	430,000	Federal Appliance Restoratoin	5.800%	04/21/25	98.000	421,400	5%	6.010%	6.010%	9.435
01/07/11	430,000	Big Blue Box	5.900%	08/20/25	101.000	434,300	5%	5.797%	5.750%	9.526
01/10/11	320,000	Wheels Corp.	7.800%	10/20/25	91.000	291,200	3%	8.904%	8.904%	8.205
Subtotal Corp	$6,344,000					$6,120,982	70%			

Government Bonds

Date	Par	Security	Coupon	Maturity	Price	Market Value	%			Duration
01/27/11	$100,000	Fed Home Loan Bank	3.550%	02/15/17	98.500	$98,500	1%	3.830%	3.830%	5.304
02/04/11	100,000	Federal Farm Credit Bank	3.780%	05/15/18	99.500	99,500	1%	3.859%	3.859%	6.257
Subtotal Govt	$200,000					$198,000	2%			

Municipal Bonds

Date	Par	Security	Coupon	Maturity	Price	Market Value	%			Duration
01/23/11	$100,000	Charleston SC Airport	0.000%	04/15/20	65.000	$65,000	1%	4.723%	2.253%	9.015
08/04/10	300,000	Hays TX Cons Indpt. Sch. Dist	4.000%	08/15/20	99.240	297,720	3%	4.093%	4.093%	8.033
08/04/10	50,000	Maryland Power Grid	4.875%	09/04/20	110.000	55,000	1%	3.679%	2.753%	7.901
09/04/10	300,000	Great State of TX GO	3.750%	03/15/21	104.500	313,500	4%	3.242%	3.027%	8.557
09/04/10	330,000	Austin Sewer District	3.875%	09/15/21	107.500	354,750	4%	3.068%	2.288%	8.874
09/04/10	100,000	Randolph County Water District	4.250%	10/31/21	108.000	108,000	1%	3.383%	3.383%	8.826
08/04/10	380,000	Shelby Cnty Tenn	4.750%	03/01/22	101.000	383,800	4%	4.637%	4.637%	8.673
02/10/11	100,000	Wisconsin State GO	4.750%	08/15/22	95.000	95,000	1%	5.337%	5.337%	8.484
02/03/11	50,000	Indiana Public Building Bonds	4.500%	12/15/22	98.000	49,000	1%	4.722%	4.688%	9.024
02/14/11	72,000	MN State Edutcation Fund	4.500%	09/15/23	85.000	61,200	1%	6.237%	6.237%	8.977
Subtotal Muni	$1,782,000					$1,782,970	20%			
Subtotal bond portfolio only						$8,101,952	92%			
Average Weighted Yields for bond portfolio only								5.690%	5.600%	
Average Weighted Duration for bond portfolio only										8.638

(Continued)

Table 11.5 (Continued)

Settlement Date	Face Value	Security	Coupon	Maturity	Purchase Price	Total Cost	% of Assets	Yield to Maturity	Yield to Worst	Modified Duration
Bond Funds										
10/21/10	N/A	Aggressive Bond Funds, Ltd.	N/A	N/A	9.270	$299,996	3%	N/A	N/A	N/A
10/21/10	N/A	Investment grade bond fund	N/A	N/A	10.000	192,000	2%	N/A	N/A	N/A
Subtotal Bond Funds	N/A					$491,996	6%			
Other Securities										
02/03/11	N/A	ProShares Long 20+ Treasury	N/A	N/A	1.000	$194,674	2%	N/A	N/A	N/A
Subtotal Other Securities	N/A					$194,674	2%			
Total Portfolio						$8,788,622	100%			

Portfolio Sensitivity

Table 11.6 shows the portfolio's sensitivity to interest rate movements. Notice how the rebalanced portfolio is positioned to take advantage of a downward trend in interest rates from its average weighted duration of 8.6 years.

Asset Reports

Asset Allocation by Type   The chart in Figure 11.1 (see p. 183) shows the rebalanced portfolio's various component allocations. As you can see, the allocation represents exactly what our targets were as we stated in the beginning of this chapter.

Asset Allocation by Region   Most of the allocation by region is national in the corporate bonds and other securities (see Figure 11.2 on p. 183). The municipal bonds allocate assets to individual states—including Texas, with the heaviest concentration at 11 percent of total assets.

Asset Allocation by Sector   The pie-chart in Figure 11.3 (see p. 183) identifies the investment sectors into which we rebalanced the portfolio. Notice that the heaviest concentrations are in healthcare, industrial, technology, utilities, and consumer cyclical sectors. These represent the sweet-spot for the economic decline.

Bond Fund Allocation   The pie-chart in Figure 11.4 (see p. 184) shows the allocation to the various bond funds the portfolio holds. Since bond funds represent just 6 percent of the overall portfolio, it is of less concern that there's an obvious undue concentration in just two funds.

Income Reports

So many investors who live on the income produced by their holdings live and die by the monthly cash flow report. Table 11.7 (see p. 185–187) shows the interest and principal cash flows from the green-shoots strategy. All totaled, this portfolio produces about $450,000 in annual cash flow with a few increases as bonds mature in the later years.

Table 11.6 Portfolio Sensitivity: Green Shoots—All Bond Portfolios

Settlement Date	Face Value	Security	Coupon	Maturity	Purchase Price	Total Cost	Yield to Worst	Call Price	Δ in Value −150 bps	Δ in Value −100 bps	Δ in Value −50 bps	Δ in Value +50 bps	Δ in Value +100 bps	Δ in Value +150 bps
Corporate Bonds														
09/03/10	$400,000	Pharmacom International	5.800%	06/15/21	102.000	$408,000	5.208%	100.000	$65,794	$46,715	$28,571	($5,108)	($20,736)	($35,612)
01/19/11	430,000	Blue Sky Computers	5.000%	03/15/22	99.940	429,742	5.006%	100.000	59,117	38,372	18,686	(17,741)	(34,590)	(50,594)
01/04/11	430,000	Auto Center Stores	5.450%	10/20/22	101.000	434,300	5.317%	100.000	61,880	40,349	19,958	(17,659)	(35,006)	(51,451)
01/14/11	214,000	Oregon Pharmaceutical Corp.	4.670%	12/20/22	96.000	205,440	5.122%	100.000	30,134	19,526	9,492	(8,983)	(17,485)	(25,536)
01/12/11	400,000	Oil Slick International	6.750%	01/25/23	91.000	364,000	7.923%	100.000	46,828	30,388	14,795	(14,042)	(27,373)	(40,034)
01/12/11	400,000	American Telecom	4.750%	02/15/23	99.000	396,000	4.860%	100.000	58,870	38,131	18,530	(17,523)	(34,098)	(49,782)
09/20/09	430,000	Laptop Computers International	5.780%	06/04/23	91.000	391,300	6.798%	100.000	58,656	37,914	18,388	(17,323)	(33,649)	(49,041)
01/15/11	400,000	Southern Power Grid	6.750%	07/20/23	96.000	384,000	7.241%	100.000	51,666	33,490	16,287	(15,426)	(30,041)	(43,892)
01/12/11	400,000	Global Burgers Corp.	5.700%	10/20/23	97.000	388,000	6.039%	100.000	56,602	36,640	17,796	(16,811)	(32,696)	(47,713)
01/11/11	400,000	AngelMed, Inc.	5.000%	09/13/24	95.000	380,000	5.500%	100.000	61,785	40,228	19,968	(16,995)	(33,851)	(49,715)
01/15/11	400,000	Deep Discount Retail Stores Federation	6.120%	10/20/24	93.000	372,000	6.915%	100.000	55,072	35,601	17,268	(16,272)	(31,610)	(46,075)

Date	Par	Name	Coupon	Maturity	Price	Cost	Yield							
01/12/11	430,000	Residential Entertainment Systems, Inc.	7.500%	11/20/24	98.000	421,400	7.736%	100.000	58,483	37,837	18,368	(17,336)	(33,704)	(49,167)
01/15/11	430,000	Operating Companies, Inc.	5.000%	01/15/25	93.000	399,900	5.734%	100.000	64,621	41,710	20,201	(18,979)	(36,818)	(53,591)
01/13/11	430,000	Federal Appliance Restoratoin	5.800%	04/21/25	98.000	421,400	13.237%	100.000	(166,284)	(176,157)	(185,486)	(202,644)	(210,535)	(218,005)
01/07/11	430,000	Big Blue Box	5.900%	08/20/25	101.000	434,300	5.750%	100.000	72,339	47,363	23,946	(18,627)	(37,975)	(56,146)
01/10/11	320,000	Wheels Corp.	7.800%	10/20/25	91.000	291,200	8.904%	100.000	40,006	25,861	12,544	(11,822)	(22,969)	(33,484)
Subtotal Corp	$6,344,000					$6,120,982			$675,569	$373,968	$89,313	($433,290)	($673,136)	($899,838)
Government Bonds														
01/27/11	$100,000	Fed Home Loan Bank	3.550%	02/15/17	98.500	$98,500	3.830%	100.000	$8,347	$5,478	$2,696	($2,614)	($5,147)	($7,604)
02/04/11	100,000	Federal Farm Credit Bank	3.780%	05/15/18	99.500	99,500	3.859%	100.000	9,954	6,514	3,197	(3,082)	(6,054)	(8,921)
Subtotal Govt	$200,000					$198,000			$18,302	$11,991	$5,893	($5,696)	($11,202)	($16,525)
Municipal Bonds														
01/23/11	$100,000	Charleston SC Airport	0.000%	04/15/20	65.000	$65,000	2.253%	100.000	$28,299	$24,113	$20,124	$12,700	$9,247	$5,956
08/04/10	300,000	Hays TX Cons Indpt. Sch. Dist	4.000%	08/15/20	99.240	297,720	4.093%	100.000	39,349	25,589	12,484	(11,895)	(23,231)	(34,036)
08/04/10	50,000	Maryland Power Grid	4.875%	09/04/20	110.000	55,000	2.753%	100.000	12,104	9,369	6,766	1,923	(328)	(2,473)
09/04/10	300,000	Great State of TX GO	3.750%	03/15/21	104.500	313,500	3.027%	101.000	53,684	37,703	22,524	(5,598)	(18,619)	(30,997)

(Continued)

Table 11.6 (Continued)

Settlement Date	Face Value	Security	Coupon	Maturity	Purchase Price	Total Cost	Yield to Worst	Call Price	Δ in Value −150 bps	Δ in Value −100 bps	Δ in Value −50 bps	Δ in Value +50 bps	Δ in Value +100 bps	Δ in Value +150 bps
09/04/10	330,000	Austin Sewer District	3.875%	09/15/21	107.500	354,750	2.288%	100.000	82,670	62,771	43,916	9,107	(6,954)	(22,185)
09/04/10	100,000	Randolph County Water District	4.250%	10/31/21	108.000	108,000	3.383%	100.000	15,718	10,195	4,961	(4,704)	(9,166)	(13,398)
08/04/10	380,000	Shelby Cnty Tenn	4.750%	03/01/22	101.000	383,800	4.637%	100.000	55,302	35,857	17,443	(16,527)	(32,190)	(47,038)
02/10/11	100,000	Wisconsin State GO	4.750%	08/15/22	95.000	95,000	5.337%	100.000	13,435	8,714	4,240	(4,020)	(7,832)	(11,448)
02/03/11	50,000	Indiana Public Building Bonds	4.500%	12/15/22	98.000	49,000	4.688%	100.000	7,438	4,872	2,446	(2,022)	(4,078)	(6,024)
02/14/11	72,000	MN State Edutcation Fund	4.500%	09/15/23	85.000	61,200	6.237%	100.000	9,192	5,950	2,889	(2,729)	(5,306)	(7,742)
Subtotal Muni	$1,782,000					$1,782,970			$317,191	$225,134	$137,793	($23,763)	($98,455)	($169,385)
Total Bond Portfolio						$8,101,952			$1,011,062	$611,093	$233,000	($462,749)	($782,793)	($1,085,748)

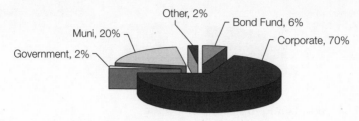

Figure 11.1   Asset Allocation by Type

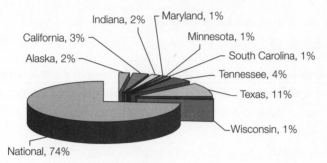

Figure 11.2   Asset Allocation by Region

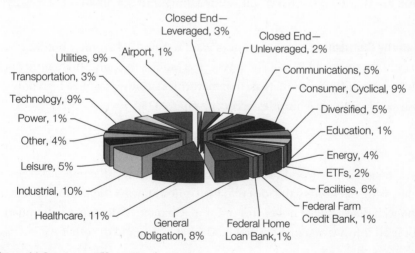

Figure 11.3   Asset Allocation by Sector

Portfolio Distribution by Coupon and Maturity   The report in Table 11.8 (see p. 188) has four sections:

1. Distribution by maturity
2. Distribution by coupon

Specialty—High Yield, 61%

Specialty—Bank Loan, 39%

Figure 11.4   Bond Fund Allocation by Sector

3. Graphic of distribution by maturity

4. Graphic of distribution by coupon

It is important to see where the concentrations of the maturities and coupons are within the portfolio. The green-shoots strategy emphasizes a longer maturity to increase the duration. As interest rates fall, this will make the portfolio more valuable.

Notice also that most of the coupons in this portfolio fall in the 5 to 7 percent range. These are the corporates on which the portfolio concentrated. They are slightly more risky, with some falling into the junk-bond category.

Maturity Distribution   Most investors want to know when their holdings will mature. The graph in Figure 11.5 (see p. 189) shows the portfolio maturity profile by year and by amount. Note that maturities steadily grow to a high point in year 2023, with no maturities occurring after 2025.

■ ■ ■

There is a new world order to the bond market. It will come as a shock to many who still hold to the idea that the United States is the world's dominant financial player. We're not of this opinion. Chapter 12 describes how America got itself into a weakened position and what China and the other Asian Tigers are likely to do about it.

■ ■ ■

Neo set down the brokerage statements he was reviewing. "Already, we have a book profit of $250,000 over what we ended the nuclear winter with."

Table 11.7 Monthly Cash Flows Green Shoots—All Portfolios

Interest Income

	2010	2011	2012	2013	2014	2015	2016	2017	2018	2019	2020
January	$0	$37,750	$37,750	$37,750	$37,750	$37,750	$37,750	$37,750	$37,750	$37,750	$37,750
February	0	32,335	32,335	32,335	32,335	32,335	32,335	32,335	30,560	30,560	30,560
March	0	44,633	44,633	44,633	44,633	44,633	44,633	44,633	44,633	44,633	44,633
April	0	60,308	60,308	60,308	60,308	60,308	60,308	60,308	60,308	60,308	60,308
May	0	20,140	20,140	20,140	20,140	20,140	20,140	20,140	20,140	18,250	18,250
June	0	30,149	30,149	30,149	30,149	30,149	30,149	30,149	30,149	30,149	30,149
July	0	37,750	37,750	37,750	37,750	37,750	37,750	37,750	37,750	37,750	37,750
August	0	32,335	32,335	32,335	32,335	32,335	32,335	30,560	30,560	30,560	30,560
September	0	44,633	44,633	44,633	44,633	44,633	44,633	44,633	44,633	44,633	44,633
October	0	60,308	60,308	60,308	60,308	60,308	60,308	60,308	60,308	60,308	60,308
November	18,015	20,140	20,140	20,140	20,140	20,140	20,140	20,140	18,250	18,250	18,250
December	30,149	30,149	30,149	30,149	30,149	30,149	30,149	30,149	30,149	30,149	30,149
Total	$48,164	$450,628	$450,628	$450,628	$450,628	$450,628	$450,628	$448,853	$445,188	$443,298	$443,298

(Continued)

Table 11.7 (Continued)

	Principal Paydowns										
	2010	2011	2012	2013	2014	2015	2016	2017	2018	2019	2020
January	$0	$0	$0	$0	$0	$0	$0	$0	$0	$0	$470,000
February	0	0	0	0	0	0	0	100,000	0	0	0
March	0	0	0	0	0	0	0	0	0	0	0
April	0	0	0	0	0	0	0	0	0	0	100,000
May	0	0	0	0	0	0	0	0	100,000	0	0
June	0	0	0	0	0	0	0	0	0	0	0
July	0	0	0	0	0	0	0	0	0	0	0
August	0	0	0	0	0	0	0	0	0	0	300,000
September	0	0	0	0	0	0	0	0	0	0	50,000
October	0	0	0	0	0	0	0	0	0	0	0
November	0	0	0	0	0	0	0	0	0	0	0
December	0	0	0	0	0	0	0	0	0	0	0
Total	$0	$0	$0	$0	$0	$0	$0	$100,000	$100,000	$0	$920,000

Total Cashflows

	2010	2011	2012	2013	2014	2015	2016	2017	2018	2019	2020
January	0	37,750	37,750	37,750	37,750	37,750	37,750	37,750	37,750	37,750	507,750
February	0	32,335	32,335	32,335	32,335	32,335	32,335	132,335	30,560	30,560	30,560
March	0	44,633	44,633	44,633	44,633	44,633	44,633	44,633	44,633	44,633	44,633
April	0	60,308	60,308	60,308	60,308	60,308	60,308	60,308	60,308	60,308	160,308
May	0	20,140	20,140	20,140	20,140	20,140	20,140	20,140	120,140	18,250	18,250
June	0	30,149	30,149	30,149	30,149	30,149	30,149	30,149	30,149	30,149	30,149
July	0	37,750	37,750	37,750	37,750	37,750	37,750	37,750	37,750	37,750	37,750
August	0	32,335	32,335	32,335	32,335	32,335	32,335	30,560	30,560	30,560	330,560
September	0	44,633	44,633	44,633	44,633	44,633	44,633	44,633	44,633	44,633	94,633
October	0	60,308	60,308	60,308	60,308	60,308	60,308	60,308	60,308	60,308	60,308
November	18,015	20,140	20,140	20,140	20,140	20,140	20,140	20,140	18,250	18,250	18,250
December	30,149	30,149	30,149	30,149	30,149	30,149	30,149	30,149	30,149	30,149	30,149
Total	**48,164**	**450,628**	**450,628**	**450,628**	**450,628**	**450,628**	**450,628**	**548,853**	**545,188**	**443,298**	**1,363,298**

Table 11.8 Portfolio Distribution by Coupon and Maturity: Green Shoots Strategy—All Bond Portfolios Only

Distribution by Maturity

Maturity	Number	Face Value	Cost	% of Assets	Weighted Average YTM	Weighted Average Coupon	Weighted Average Duration
< 1 Year	0	0K	0K	0%	0.0%	0.0%	0.00
1 – 3 Years	0	0K	0K	0%	0.0%	0.0%	0.00
3 – 5 Years	0	0K	0K	0%	0.0%	0.0%	0.00
5 – 7 Years	1	100K	99K	1%	3.8%	3.6%	5.30
7 – 10 Years	4	550K	517K	6%	4.1%	3.5%	7.80
> 10 Years	23	7.7M	7.5M	92%	5.8%	5.6%	8.74

Distribution by Coupon

Coupon	Number	Face Value	Cost	% of Assets	Weighted Average YTM	Weighted Average Coupon	Weighted Average Duration
Under 3%	1	100K	65K	1%	4.7%	0.0%	9.01
3% – 5%	13	2.5M	2.5M	31%	4.1%	4.3%	8.45
5% – 7%	12	5.0M	4.8M	59%	6.1%	5.7%	8.78
7% – 10%	2	750K	713K	9%	8.2%	7.6%	8.31
Over 10%	0	0K	0K	0%	0.0%	0.0%	0.00

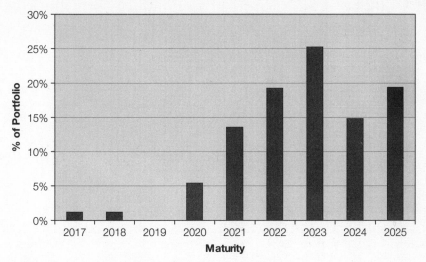

Figure 11.5   Maturity Distribution—All Portfolios

El Greedo nodded. "So what else is there to do?"

Neo stood and slid his jacket off the back of his chair. "Let's go, my over-stressed relative."

"Where to?"

"Shopping. I figure it's time to get you out of that pea-soup-green Kia—"

"We're not dipping into our principal."

"Don't have to. I have a modest interest in a BMW dealership and leasing operation. We can afford it. Say, El, answer me one question. Why do you do this investing thing?"

El Greedo stopped and looked his brother-in-law in the eye. "If I didn't do this investing thing, who would have saved our family's nest egg?"

Chapter 12

THE NEW BOND WORLD ORDER

United States: No Longer the World's Economic Force

The United States suffers from a self-inflicted debt burden that is crushing our financial resources. Our nanny-state mentality requires our national debt to increase year in and year out. An almost-bankrupt Social Security system, Medicare run wild, unfunded pension liabilities, and government budget deficits are the result. Unless the United States stops doing everything for major segments of its population from cradle to grave, digging out from under our debt will be impossible.

America's Unhappy Investor

As of October 2010, China had $2.6 trillion in foreign exchange reserves. The majority of these reserves are in dollar-denominated assets. As long as the United States debt problem persists, the U.S. dollar will continue to depreciate. This leaves China a most unhappy investor. Connecting the dots, this leaves the U.S. dollar and bond market in the most vulnerable position ever.

China: The Biggest Bond Vigilante

China and the other Asian Tigers lead the world's economy. The United States relies on China to buy our Treasurys. That is how we're currently financing our massive debt and budget deficits. The fact is, one day China will no longer need to buy foreign investments such as U.S. Treasurys. A more beneficial and profitable investment of their Yuan will be internal use for their own economy.

Therein lies the danger to the United States. China has made it clear that they do not approve of the massive U.S. debt. We aren't sure the U.S. government is listening. Witness the U.S. Congress drafting a resolution to ask China to please not manipulate their currency to the detriment of the United States. This single act humiliated the United States on the world's financial stage. It demonstrated just how fiscally ignorant our leaders really are.

The United States has placed China in the position of being able to exert more economic force than even the worst bond vigilantes. They will likely begin using that muscle at some point in the future. At worst, they will stop buying U.S. Treasurys. At best, they will drastically reduce their purchases. Either way, the consequences will be the largest interest rate hikes in history and, with that, an enormous increase in U.S. debt.

The Three Stages of the Bond Market

We have described the three stages of the bond market throughout this book:

1. *Triage stage*, when the bond market turns south and heads into a bear market direction
2. *Nuclear winter*, an extended time when the bond bear is at its ugliest

3. *Green shoots*, when the bond market begins to prosper once again and the general economy weakens.

Depending on how the United States deals with the New Bond World Order, we may find ourselves mired in one stage or another. On the other hand, perhaps this crisis will force America to reemerge as the resilient country we are known to be—a country filled with resourceful people. We elect leaders who are intelligent, well-intentioned individuals. They will eventually get the message about fiscal responsibility. When they do and when they make the changes needed to begin repairing our finances, the general economy and the bond market will peacefully coexist.

However, until that time we see the economy ramping up, interest rates rising, and a coming bond bear market sometime in the near future. We could be wrong. The economy could experience a deflationary spiral like Japan. We think this is certainly possible, though less likely. Even so, it would still mean a nuclear winter for the bond market. The techniques and strategies identified in this book will still be applicable.

The Final Solution

Stating the solution is simple: The United States must become more self-financing and less dependent on China, the UK, Japan, and others to finance our debt. Doing the things necessary to make this a reality is difficult. It first requires electing officials willing to make the necessary decisions regardless of how it affects their chances for reelection. They must cut spending.

Should we be proven wrong about the New Bond World Order, what you have learned between these pages is how to proactively and methodically strategize portfolio changes into what can go right and wrong in the bond market. We have given you the tools so you no longer have to rely on the shoot-from-the-hip methods most individual investors use. Rather, you now have the tools and economic indicators to formulate a logical and profitable management program for your bond portfolio—regardless of the economic cycle.

Along with that, we've provided you with a simple-to-use automated e-workbook that takes you through the management of your bond portfolio. We hope that you will follow the instructions for downloading the Excel template to your personal computer. The simple directions for its use are in the appendix.

We hope that you have enjoyed reading this book. We also hope that El Greedo and Neo taught you something through their evolving, though sometimes fumbling, trading strategy.

Our best wishes to you,

MARILYN COHEN & CHRIS MALBURG

AUTOMATED E-WORKBOOK INSTRUCTIONS

We have included a complimentary automated e-workbook. It is free of charge and comes with the purchase of this book. This is the same e-workbook used throughout the text. It employs an Excel spreadsheet. You must have Excel on your computer, but you do not have to know much about Excel to expertly operate the e-workbook. We've strived to make it as user-friendly as possible.

We hope that you will download the e-workbook and use it as one of the tools for managing your bond portfolio.

Downloading Instructions

1. This e-workbook requires the use of Excel. If you do not have Excel on your computer, you will need to get it. However, you do not have to know how to use Excel to operate the e-workbook.

2. Go to http://www.SurvivingTheBondBearMarket.com.

3. Click on the *Download Automated E-Workbook* button and follow the instructions.

4. The procedure asks for your authorizing password. Your password that authorizes your access and download is:

NuclearWinter

5. Next, the system will ask where in your computer you want the Automated Workbook files to go. Save the file to your computer.

6. Click *Download E-Workbook*. The zip file containing the e-workbook templates will automatically download to the location you specified. The zip file contains:

   a. Instruction manual and automated tutorial video

   b. The e-workbook containing a blank portfolio

   c. The e-workbook containing the Triage portfolio appearing in the book

   d. The e-workbook containing the Nuclear Winter portfolio appearing in the book

   e. The e-workbook containing the Green-Shoots portfolio appearing in the book

7. Proceed from here to launch whichever workbook version you wish.

Launching the E-Workbook

1. Launch Excel on you computer, then open the e-workbook file, or double-click directly on the e-workbook file and Excel will open automatically just like any Excel file.

2. A message will likely appear asking if you wish to enable macros. Click on the *Enable Macros* button. Some computers have their security options set to deny macros on Excel files. If this is the case for your computer, follow these directions:

a. In Excel, enter Tools.

b. Click on Macros.

c. Click on Security.

d. Click on Macro Security.

e. Click on Medium security level.

f. Press OK to exit all of the Excel Tools.

Your macros on the automated e-workbook will now run.

3. The e-workbook will launch from here and land on the cover page.
4. Click on the Portfolio tab in the lower-left corner. You are now in the e-workbook's dashboard and can navigate around the system wherever you wish.

Loading and Editing Portfolio Positions

The automated e-workbook loads all portfolio positions and edits existing positions from the *Current Portfolio* button. Clicking this button brings you directly to the Current Portfolio screen.

If you loaded the **Green-Shoots** portfolio and brought up the portfolio screen using the instructions above, the first position you see is Aggressive Bond Funds.

Add New Positions

Press the *Add New Position* button on the right to insert new positions into your portfolio. A comprehensive screen including popup menus for various items appears. Simply complete the information requested for each new position. Be as accurate and complete as possible. When done entering each position, press the *Save* button. The new position will be saved and the workbook returns you to the *Current Portfolio* screen.

Edit Existing Positions

It's easy to make changes to existing positions. From the *Current Portfolio* screen, just double-click on the position you wish to edit. The system takes you to the edit screen for that particular position. Let's try it. Double-click on the second position in the *Current Portfolio* screen, American Telecom. From the new edit screen appearing you may change any part of this security or delete it entirely. When finished editing, press *Update Bond*. The system will save your changes and take you back to the *Current Portfolio* screen.

Import Portfolios

You may wish to import an entirely new portfolio into your e-workbook or add on another portfolio. Begin this process by:

1. Pressing the *Import Portfolio* button. A menu screen appears asking if you want to replace the existing portfolio.
2. Be careful. A *Yes* answer will overwrite the existing portfolio, completely replacing it.
3. A *No* answer will append the new portfolio to the existing one. This feature is useful for adding entire portfolios, perhaps from other trading platforms.
4. Once the operation is completed, the system returns you to the *Current Portfolio* screen.

Viewing and Isolating Categories

We included three filters in the *Current Portfolio* screen on the right side for managing your portfolio. Here's how to use them.

Name Filter   Often you will have several positions from the same bond issuer. The Name Filter allows you to see just the positions from that issuer. Enter the issuer's name. Those positions will appear on the screen. To reinstate the entire portfolio on the screen, just delete your *Name Filter* request.

CUSIP Filter   You may be searching for a particular position. This can be an arduous task for a large portfolio. If you know the CUSIP number, enter it in the *CUSIP Filter* box and that security will appear. To reinstate the entire portfolio on the screen, just delete the *CUSIP Filter* request.

Portfolio   The *Portfolio Filter* features a drop-down menu showing all the portfolio trading platforms you have entered for each position. These are the brokerage firms where the positions are kept. If you wish to see all the positions you have at a particular broker, select that broker's name from the drop-down menu. The positions will appear on the *Edit Portfolio* screen. To reinstate the entire portfolio on the screen, select *Show All* from the drop-down menu.

Try it. Select E-trade from the drop-down menu screen. Just the positions at the E-Trade brokerage appear. There are nine, beginning with Austin Sewer District. To go back to the whole portfolio listing, select *Show All* from the drop-down menu.

Positions to Display

A true convenience is the ability to isolate various categories of positions, including municipal bonds, corporates, governments, funds, and other types. To show just municipal bonds, for example, press the button to the left of municipal bonds. All the munis appear on the screen. To reinstate the entire portfolio on the screen, just press the *Show All* button. You can follow this same procedure for all the other categories of positions.

Filters Across the Top

For added ease of sorting through your portfolio we've added six additional filters across the top. To use them, just click on the circle to the left of each. The *Current Portfolio* screen sorts by the criteria you just selected. The filters across the top include:

- *Sort by Name:* Lists the securities in alphabetical order
- *Sort by Face Value:* Lists the securities in order of lowest face value to highest
- *Sort by CUSIP number:* Lists the securities in order of lowest CUSIP number to highest
- *Sort by Type:* Lists securities by type in alphabetical order
- *Sort by Coupon:* Lists the securities in order of lowest coupon to highest
- *Sort by Maturity:* Lists the securities in order of earliest maturity to latest

Leaving the Current Portfolio Screen

To leave the *Current Portfolio* screen and return to the main system dashboard, just click on the red X in the upper-right corner. The dashboard appears.

Reports

The most useful part of this e-workbook is its user-friendly reporting. With the reports, you can dissect any part of your portfolio, see its sensitivity to movements in interest rates, and fine-tune duration. Here is how to operate the e-workbook's reporting system:

Entering the Reporting System

From the dashboard, click on *Run Reports*. The report menu appears.

Managing Reports

When you enter the report main menu, you will see the *Select Portfolio* box at the top with a drop-down menu. This feature allows to you report all positions or positions from any of the trading platforms that you entered.

Then, in the lower right, there is a box to either check or not, entitled, *Return to Report Menu*. We included this as a convenience to you. It tells the system that you wish to return to the report menu after you exit a particular report. If you don't check it, the system will return you to the system dashboard after exiting a particular report. We prefer keeping it checked—but that's just our preference for using the system.

Asset Reports

There are two types of asset reports: asset allocation and a separate asset report for bond funds.

Asset Allocation   Click on *Asset Allocation*, and then click on *Generate Reports*. The first Asset Allocation report appears as a pie-chart. Within the Asset Allocation, there are four different reports:

- Asset allocation, other
- Asset allocation by region: This is useful to determine geographic concentration
- Asset allocation by security sector: Use this report to identify concentrations in various types of securities
- Asset allocation type: This report tells you the concentration in the five types of security categories: Munis, corporates, governments, funds, and other.

To move between types of reports, click on the identifying tab in the lower-left corner.

Once your chosen report appears, you have the option of:

- Printing it as you would any Excel report.
- Saving it to its own Excel file.
- Discarding it. To discard the report, click on the small X in the upper-left corner. The system asks you if you wish to save the changes you made (that is, to save the report). It then allows you to identify the location where you want it saved and the file name. If you don't wish to save the report, click *No*. The e-workbook then takes you back to the report menu (if you checked that little box we spoke of earlier).

For example, Figure A.1 shows the Asset Allocation by Sector for the Green-Shoots portfolio. See if you can show it using the instructions above.

Bond Funds Since bond funds are a peculiar category different from individual bonds, we separated them with their own reports. From the Asset Reports menu, select Bond Funds. The e-workbook takes you to the bond fund reports. There are four tabs in the lower-left corner for the different bond reports:

1. Sector
2. Region

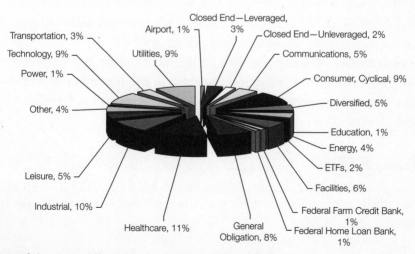

Figure A.1   Asset Allocation by Sector—All Portfolios

3. Type
4. A complete listing of all bond funds entered in the portfolio

Printing, saving, and exiting the bond fund section works exactly as it does above in the Asset Allocation reports. Table A.1 shows the Bond Fund listing from the Green-Shoots portfolio. See if you can duplicate it in your e-workbook.

Income Reports

We included three different types of income reports:

1. Cash flows
2. Maturity distribution
3. Coupon maturity

Within each report type there are different reports available.

Cash Flows   To open the Cash Flow reports, click on *Cash Flows*, and then click on *Generate Reports*. The cash flow report will appear. This report shows cash flows from the portfolio three ways:

1. Cash flow from interest
2. Cash flow from maturities
3. Total cash flow

The e-workbook arrays the cash flows by month and year. Using this report, it is easy to see exactly when over the next 10 years your portfolio will generate cash and from where (interest or principal repayment).

To exit the cash flow report, click on the small X in the upper-right corner. You will be prompted to either save the report or not. If you don't wish to save the report, the e-workbook takes you back to the report menu. Table A.2 is the Cash Flow report for the Green-Shoots portfolio.

Maturity Distribution   This is a graphic display of the positions in the portfolio. It shows not only when they mature by year but the percentage of the portfolio that is maturing in any given year. Use this report to determine maturity concentrations by year.

Table A.1 Bond Fund Appraisal—All Portfolios

Settlement Date	Shares Purchased	Security	Bond Fund Type	Bond Fund Sector	Bond Fund State	Purchase Price	Total Cost	% of Assets
Bond Funds								
10/21/10	32,362	Aggressive Bond Funds, Ltd.	Closed End— Leveraged	Specialty—High Yield	CALIFORNIA	9.270	299,996	61%
10/21/10	19,200	Investment grade bond fund	Closed End— Unleveraged	Specialty—Bank Loan	ALASKA	10.000	192,000	39%
Total Portfolio							491,996	100%

Table A.2 Monthly Cash Flows: Green Shoots Strategy—All Portfolios

	Interest Income										
	2010	2011	2012	2013	2014	2015	2016	2017	2018	2019	2020
January	$0	$37,750	$37,750	$37,750	$37,750	$37,750	$37,750	$37,750	$37,750	$37,750	$37,750
February	0	32,335	32,335	32,335	32,335	32,335	32,335	32,335	30,560	30,560	30,560
March	0	44,633	44,633	44,633	44,633	44,633	44,633	44,633	44,633	44,633	44,633
April	0	60,308	60,308	60,308	60,308	60,308	60,308	60,308	60,308	60,308	60,308
May	0	20,140	20,140	20,140	20,140	20,140	20,140	20,140	20,140	18,250	18,250
June	0	30,149	30,149	30,149	30,149	30,149	30,149	30,149	30,149	30,149	30,149
July	0	37,750	37,750	37,750	37,750	37,750	37,750	37,750	37,750	37,750	37,750
August	0	32,335	32,335	32,335	32,335	32,335	32,335	32,335	30,560	30,560	30,560
September	0	44,633	44,633	44,633	44,633	44,633	44,633	44,633	44,633	44,633	44,633
October	0	60,308	60,308	60,308	60,308	60,308	60,308	60,308	60,308	60,308	60,308
November	0	20,140	20,140	20,140	20,140	20,140	20,140	20,140	18,250	18,250	18,250
December	30,149	30,149	30,149	30,149	30,149	30,149	30,149	30,149	30,149	30,149	30,149
Total	$30,149	$450,628	$450,628	$450,628	$450,628	$450,628	$450,628	$448,853	$445,188	$443,298	$443,298

Principal Paydowns

	2010	2011	2012	2013	2014	2015	2016	2017	2018	2019	2020
January	$0	$0	$0	$0	$0	$0	$0	$0	$0	$0	$194,674
February	0	0	0	0	0	0	0	100,000	0	0	0
March	0	0	0	0	0	0	0	0	0	0	0
April	0	0	0	0	0	0	0	0	0	0	100,000
May	0	0	0	0	0	0	0	0	100,000	0	0
June	0	0	0	0	0	0	0	0	0	0	0
July	0	0	0	0	0	0	0	0	0	0	0
August	0	0	0	0	0	0	0	0	0	0	300,000
September	0	0	0	0	0	0	0	0	0	0	50,000
October	0	0	0	0	0	0	0	0	0	0	0
November	0	0	0	0	0	0	0	0	0	0	0
December	0	0	0	0	0	0	0	0	0	0	0
Total	**$0**	**$0**	**$0**	**$0**	**$0**	**$0**	**$0**	**$100,000**	**$100,000**	**$0**	**$644,674**

(Continued)

Table A.2 (Continued)

	2010	2011	2012	2013	2014	2015	2016	2017	2018	2019	2020
						Total Cashflows					
January	0	37,750	37,750	37,750	37,750	37,750	37,750	37,750	37,750	37,750	232,424
February	0	32,335	32,335	32,335	32,335	32,335	32,335	132,335	30,560	30,560	30,560
March	0	44,633	44,633	44,633	44,633	44,633	44,633	44,633	44,633	44,633	44,633
April	0	60,308	60,308	60,308	60,308	60,308	60,308	60,308	60,308	60,308	160,308
May	0	20,140	20,140	20,140	20,140	20,140	20,140	20,140	120,140	18,250	18,250
June	0	30,149	30,149	30,149	30,149	30,149	30,149	30,149	30,149	30,149	30,149
July	0	37,750	37,750	37,750	37,750	37,750	37,750	37,750	37,750	37,750	37,750
August	0	32,335	32,335	32,335	32,335	32,335	32,335	30,560	30,560	30,560	330,560
September	0	44,633	44,633	44,633	44,633	44,633	44,633	44,633	44,633	44,633	94,633
October	0	60,308	60,308	60,308	60,308	60,308	60,308	60,308	60,308	60,308	60,308
November	0	20,140	20,140	20,140	20,140	20,140	20,140	20,140	18,250	18,250	18,250
December	30,149	30,149	30,149	30,149	30,149	30,149	30,149	30,149	30,149	30,149	30,149
Total	**30,149**	**450,628**	**450,628**	**450,628**	**450,628**	**450,628**	**450,628**	**548,853**	**545,188**	**443,298**	**1,087,972**

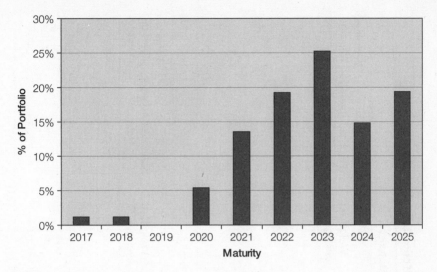

Figure A.2   Maturity Distribution—All Portfolios

As always, exit this report by clicking on the small X in the upper-right corner. You'll be prompted to either save the report or not. Then you'll be returned to the report menu. We've printed the Maturity Distribution report for the Green-Shoots portfolio in Figure A.2.

Coupon/Maturity Report   This useful report shows the portfolio's distribution by both maturity and coupon. We present it as both tables and bar graphs. Use the distribution by maturity to determine concentration in various maturity buckets. Likewise, use the distribution by coupon to determine concentration in various coupon categories.

Exit this report by clicking on the small X in the upper-right corner. You'll be prompted to either save the report or not. Then you'll be returned to the report menu. Table A.3 shows the Coupon/Maturity report for the Green-Shoots portfolio.

Other Reports

This innocently labeled category is quite likely the most useful set of reports. These provide an array of vital information for each category of the portfolio,

Table A.3 Portfolio Distribution by Coupon and Maturity—All Bond Portfolio Only

Distribution by Maturity

Maturity	Number	Face Value	Cost	% of Assets	Weighted Average YTM	Weighted Average Coupon	Weighted Average Duration
<1 Year	0	0K	0K	0%	0.0%	0.0%	0.00
1–3 Years	0	0K	0K	0%	0.0%	0.0%	0.00
3–5 Years	0	0K	0K	0%	0.0%	0.0%	0.00
5–7 Years	1	100K	99K	1%	3.8%	3.6%	5.30
7–10 Years	4	550K	517K	6%	4.1%	3.5%	7.80
>10 Years	23	7.7M	7.5M	92%	5.8%	5.6%	8.74

Distribution by Coupon

Coupon	Number	Face Value	Cost	% of Assets	Weighted Average YTM	Weighted Average Coupon	Weighted Average Duration
Under 3%	1	100K	65K	1%	4.7%	0.0%	9.01
3%–5%	13	2.5M	2.5M	31%	4.2%	4.3%	8.44
5%–7%	12	5.0M	4.8M	59%	6.1%	5.7%	8.78
7%–10%	2	750K	713K	9%	8.2%	7.6%	8.31
Over 10%	0	0K	0K	0%	0.0%	0.0%	0.00

position by position. Remember in the book how El Greedo and Neo adjusted their portfolio duration to first survive the nuclear winter and then later to profit from the green shoots? These are the reports they used to do it.

Portfolio Appraisal Report   This report illustrates each position by category. If you are managing the portfolio and need to see an individual security's coupon, maturity, purchase cost, yields, and duration, this is the report for you. Additionally, it runs a total for the entire portfolio as well as the percentage of total assets for each position. Table A.4 shows the Portfolio Appraisal report for the Green-Shoots portfolio.

Exit this report the same way as all the others, by clicking on the small X in the upper-right corner. You'll be prompted to either save the report or not. Then you'll be returned to the report menu.

Sensitivity Report   To access the Sensitivity Report, click on *Sensitivity Report*. This report illustrates potential gains and losses in the portfolio as interest rates go up or down. It includes only interest rate–sensitive positions such as municipal bonds, corporate bonds, and government bonds. ETFs and the various categories of other securities are excluded from this report. The Sensitivity Report for the Green-Shoots portfolio is shown in Table A.5.

Exit this report the same way as all the others, by clicking on the small X in the upper-right corner. You'll be prompted to either save the report or not. Then you'll be returned to the report menu.

Equations

Some more quantitatively oriented readers may wish to know the equations the automated e-workbook uses to compute duration and sensitivity. These come directly from Excel's preprogrammed financial investment formulas. Here they are:

Duration

It was Frederick Macaulay who developed the concept of duration, equating it to the average time to maturity or the time required to receive half of the present value, discounted by the bond's yield to maturity, of the bond's cash flow.

Table A.4 Portfolio Appraisal With Yield to Words—All Portfolios

Settlement Date	Face Value	Security	Coupon	Maturity	Purchase Price	Total Cost	% of Assets	Yield to Maturity	Yield to Worst	Modified Duration
Corporate Bonds										
09/03/10	$400,000	Pharmacom International	5.800%	06/15/21	102.000	$408,000	5%	5.550%	5.208%	7.879
01/19/11	430,000	Blue Sky Computers	5.000%	03/15/22	99.940	429,742	5%	5.006%	5.006%	8.329
01/04/11	430,000	Auto Center Stores	5.450%	10/20/22	101.000	434,300	5%	5.334%	5.317%	8.546
01/14/11	214,000	Oregon Pharmaceutical Corp.	4.670%	12/20/22	96.000	205,440	2%	5.122%	5.122%	8.959
01/12/11	400,000	Oil Slick International	6.750%	01/25/23	91.000	364,000	4%	7.923%	7.923%	7.655
01/12/11	400,000	American Telecom	4.750%	02/15/23	99.000	396,000	5%	4.860%	4.860%	8.924
09/20/09	430,000	Laptop Computers Internat'l	5.780%	06/04/23	91.000	391,300	4%	6.798%	6.798%	8.953
01/15/11	400,000	Southern Power Grid	6.750%	07/20/23	96.000	384,000	4%	7.241%	7.241%	7.981
01/12/11	400,000	Global Burgers Corp.	5.700%	10/20/23	97.000	388,000	4%	6.039%	6.039%	8.796
01/11/11	400,000	AngelMed, Inc.	5.000%	09/13/24	95.000	380,000	4%	5.525%	5.500%	9.526
01/15/11	400,000	Deep Discount Retail Stores Federation	6.120%	10/20/24	93.000	372,000	4%	6.915%	6.915%	8.872
01/12/11	430,000	Residential Entertainment Systems, Inc.	7.500%	11/20/24	98.000	421,400	5%	7.736%	7.736%	8.375
01/15/11	430,000	Operating Companies, Inc.	5.000%	01/15/25	93.000	399,900	5%	5.734%	5.734%	9.791
01/13/11	430,000	Federal Appliance Restoration	5.800%	04/21/25	98.000	421,400	5%	6.010%	6.010%	9.435
01/07/11	430,000	Big Blue Box	5.900%	08/20/25	101.000	434,300	5%	5.797%	5.750%	9.526
01/10/11	320,000	Wheels Corp.	7.800%	10/20/25	91.000	291,200	3%	8.904%	8.904%	8.205
Subtotal Corp	$6,344,000					$6,120,982	70%			

Government Bonds

			Coupon	Maturity	Price	Market Value	%			
01/27/11	$100,000	Fed Home Loan Bank	3.550%	02/15/17	98.500	$98,500	1%	3.830%	3.830%	5.304
02/04/11	100,000	Federal Farm Credit Bank	3.780%	05/15/18	99.500	99,500	1%	3.859%	3.859%	6.257
Subtotal Govt	$200,000					$198,000	2%			

Municipal Bonds

01/23/11	$100,000	Charleston SC Airport	0.000%	04/15/20	65.000	$65,000	1%	4.723%	2.253%	9.015
08/04/10	300,000	Hays TX Cons Indpt. Sch. Dist	4.000%	08/15/20	99.240	297,720	3%	4.093%	4.093%	8.033
08/04/10	50,000	Maryland Power Grid	4.875%	09/04/20	110.000	55,000	1%	3.679%	2.753%	7.901
09/04/10	300,000	Great State of TX GO	3.750%	03/15/21	104.500	313,500	4%	3.242%	3.027%	8.557
09/04/10	330,000	Austin Sewer District	3.875%	09/15/21	107.500	354,750	4%	3.068%	2.288%	8.874
09/04/10	100,000	Randolph County Water District	4.250%	10/31/21	108.000	108,000	1%	3.383%	3.383%	8.826
08/04/10	380,000	Shelby Cnty Tenn	4.750%	03/01/22	101.000	383,800	4%	4.637%	4.637%	8.673
02/10/11	100,000	Wisconsin State GO	4.750%	08/15/22	95.000	95,000	1%	5.337%	5.337%	8.484
02/03/11	50,000	Indiana Public Building Bonds	4.500%	12/15/22	98.000	49,000	1%	4.722%	4.688%	9.024
02/14/11	72,000	MN State Education Fund	4.500%	09/15/23	85.000	61,200	1%	6.237%	6.237%	8.977
Subtotal Muni	$1,782,000					$1,782,970	20%			
Subtotal bond portfolio only						$8,101,952	92%			
Average Weighted Yields for bond portfolio only								5.690%	5.600%	

(Continued)

Table A.4 (Continued)

Settlement Date	Face Value	Security	Coupon	Maturity	Purchase Price	Total Cost	% of Assets	Yield to Maturity	Yield to Worst	Modified Duration
Average Weighted Duration for bond portfolio only										8.638
Bond Funds										
10/21/10	$32,362	Aggressive Bond Funds, Ltd.	N/A	N/A	9.270	$299,996	3%	N/A	N/A	N/A
10/21/10	19,200	Investment grade bond fund	N/A	N/A	10.000	192,000	2%	N/A	N/A	N/A
Subtotal Bond Funds	$51,562					$491,996	6%			
Other Securities										
02/03/11	$470,000	ProShares Long 20+ Treasury	N/A	N/A	41.420	$194,674	2%	N/A	N/A	N/A
Subtotal Other Securities	$470,000					$194,674	2%			
Total Portfolio						$8,788,622	100%			

Table A.5 Portfolio Sensitivity—All Bond Portfolios Only

Settlement Date	Face Value	Security	Coupon	Maturity	Purchase Price	Total Cost	Yield to Worst	Call Price	Δ in Value −150 bps	Δ in Value −100 bps	Δ in Value −50 bps	Δ in Value +50 bps	Δ in Value +100 bps	Δ in Value +150 bps
Corporate Bonds														
09/03/10	$400,000	Pharmacom International	5.800%	06/15/21	102.000	$408,000	5.208%	100.000	$65,794	$46,715	$28,571	($5,108)	($20,736)	($35,612)
01/19/11	430,000	Blue Sky Computers	5.000%	03/15/22	99.940	429,742	5.006%	100.000	59,117	38,372	18,686	(17,741)	(34,590)	(50,594)
01/04/11	430,000	Auto Center Stores	5.450%	10/20/22	101.000	434,300	5.317%	100.000	61,880	40,349	19,958	(17,659)	(35,006)	(51,451)
01/14/11	214,000	Oregon Pharmaceutical Corp.	4.670%	12/20/22	96.000	205,440	5.122%	100.000	30,134	19,526	9,492	(8,983)	(17,485)	(25,536)
01/12/11	400,000	Oil Slick International	6.750%	01/25/23	91.000	364,000	7.923%	100.000	46,828	30,388	14,795	(14,042)	(27,373)	(40,034)
01/12/11	400,000	American Telecom	4.750%	02/15/23	99.000	396,000	4.860%	100.000	58,870	38,131	18,530	(17,523)	(34,098)	(49,782)
09/20/09	430,000	Laptop Computers Internat'l	5.780%	06/04/23	91.000	391,300	6.798%	100.000	58,656	37,914	18,388	(17,323)	(33,649)	(49,041)
01/15/11	400,000	Southern Power Grid	6.750%	07/20/23	96.000	384,000	7.241%	100.000	51,666	33,490	16,287	(15,426)	(30,041)	(43,892)
01/12/11	400,000	Global Burgers Corp.	5.700%	10/20/23	97.000	388,000	6.039%	100.000	56,602	36,640	17,796	(16,811)	(32,696)	(47,713)
01/11/11	400,000	AngelMed, Inc.	5.000%	09/13/24	95.000	380,000	5.500%	100.000	61,785	40,228	19,968	(16,995)	(33,851)	(49,715)
01/15/11	400,000	Deep Discount Retail Stores Federation	6.120%	10/20/24	93.000	372,000	6.915%	100.000	55,072	35,601	17,268	(16,272)	(31,610)	(46,075)

(Continued)

Table A.5 (Continued)

Settlement Date	Face Value	Security	Coupon	Maturity	Purchase Price	Total Cost	Yield to Worst	Call Price	Δ in Value −150 bps	Δ in Value −100 bps	Δ in Value −50 bps	Δ in Value +50 bps	Δ in Value +100 bps	Δ in Value +150 bps
01/12/11	430,000	Residential Entertainment Systems, Inc.	7.500%	11/20/24	98.000	421,400	7.736%	100.000	58,483	37,837	18,368	(17,336)	(33,704)	(49,167)
01/15/11	430,000	Operating Companies, Inc.	5.000%	01/15/25	93.000	399,900	5.734%	100.000	64,621	41,710	20,201	(18,979)	(36,818)	(53,591)
01/13/11	430,000	Federal Appliance Restoration	5.800%	04/21/25	98.000	421,400	13.237%	100.000	(166,284)	(176,157)	(185,486)	(202,644)	(210,535)	(218,005)
01/07/11	430,000	Big Blue Box	5.900%	08/20/25	101.000	434,300	5.750%	100.000	72,339	47,363	23,946	(18,627)	(37,975)	(56,146)
01/10/11	320,000	Wheels Corp.	7.800%	10/20/25	91.000	291,200	8.904%	100.000	40,006	25,861	12,544	(11,822)	(22,969)	(33,484)
Subtotal Corp	$6,344,000					$6,120,982			$675,569	$373,968	$89,313	($433,290)	($673,136)	($899,838)
Government Bonds														
01/27/11	$100,000	Fed Home Loan Bank	3.550%	02/15/17	98.500	$98,500	3.830%	100.000	$8,347	$5,478	$2,696	($2,614)	($5,147)	($7,604)
02/04/11	100,000	Federal Farm Credit Bank	3.780%	05/15/18	99.500	99,500	3.859%	100.000	9,954	6,514	3,197	(3,082)	(6,054)	(8,921)
Subtotal Govt	$200,000					$198,000			$18,302	$11,991	$5,893	($5,696)	($11,202)	($16,525)

Municipal Bonds

01/23/11	$100,000	Charleston SC Airport	0.000%	04/15/20	65.000	$65,000	2.253%	100.000	$28,299	$24,113	$20,124	$12,700	$9,247	$5,956
08/04/10	300,000	Hays TX Cons Indpt. Sch. Dist	4.000%	08/15/20	99.240	297,720	4.093%	100.000	39,349	25,589	12,484	(11,895)	(23,231)	(34,036)
08/04/10	50,000	Maryland Power Grid	4.875%	09/04/20	110.000	55,000	2.753%	100.000	12,104	9,369	6,766	1,923	(328)	(2,473)
09/04/10	300,000	Great State of TX GO	3.750%	03/15/21	104.500	313,500	3.027%	101.000	53,684	37,703	22,524	(5,598)	(18,619)	(30,997)
09/04/10	330,000	Austin Sewer District	3.875%	09/15/21	107.500	354,750	2.288%	100.000	82,670	62,771	43,916	9,107	(6,954)	(22,185)
09/04/10	100,000	Randolph County Water District	4.250%	10/31/21	108.000	108,000	3.383%	100.000	15,718	10,195	4,961	(4,704)	(9,166)	(13,398)
08/04/10	380,000	Shelby Cnty Tenn	4.750%	03/01/22	101.000	383,800	4.637%	100.000	55,302	35,857	17,443	(16,527)	(32,190)	(47,038)
02/10/11	100,000	Wisconsin State GO	4.750%	08/15/22	95.000	95,000	5.337%	100.000	13,435	8,714	4,240	(4,020)	(7,832)	(11,448)
02/03/11	50,000	Indiana Public Building Bonds	4.500%	12/15/22	98.000	49,000	4.688%	100.000	7,438	4,872	2,446	(2,022)	(4,078)	(6,024)
02/14/11	72,000	MN State Edutcation Fund	4.500%	09/15/23	85.000	61,200	6.237%	100.000	9,192	5,950	2,889	(2,729)	(5,306)	(7,742)
Subtotal Muni	$1,782,000					$1,782,970			$317,191	$225,134	$137,793	($23,763)	($98,455)	($169,385)
Total Bond Portfolio						$8,101,952			$1,011,062	$611,093	$233,000	($462,749)	($782,793)	($1,085,748)

The *Macaulay duration* is calculated by first calculating the weighted average of each cash flow at time *t* by the following formula:

$$w_t = \frac{CF_t / (1+y)^t}{Bond\ Price}$$

where:

w_t = weighted average of cash flow at time *t*
CF_t = cash flow at time *t*
y = yield to maturity

Then these weighted averages are summed:

Macaulay Duration Formula:

$$Macaulay\ Duration = \sum_{t=1}^{T} t \times w_t$$

where:

T = number of cash flow periods

Hence, the Macaulay duration measures the effective maturity of a bond, and can also be used to calculate the average maturity of a portfolio of fixed-income securities.

Modified Duration   *Modified duration* is a modification of the Macaulay duration to estimate interest rate risk, calculating the change in a bond's price to a change in its yield to maturity by the following formula:

Modified Duration Formula:

$$D_m = \frac{D_{Mac}}{1+y/k}$$

where:
D_m = modified duration
D_{Mac} = Macaulay duration

y = yield to maturity

k = number of payments per year

The modified duration formula is valid only when the change in yield will not alter the cash flow of the bond, such as may occur, for instance, if the price change for a callable bond increases the likelihood that it will be called.

It is also valid only for small changes in yield, because duration itself changes as the yield changes. It is a first derivative of the price-yield curve, which is a line tangent to the curve at the current price-yield point.

Duration and Modified Duration Formulas for Bonds Using Microsoft Excel

Duration = DURATION(settlement,maturity,coupon,yield, frequency, basis).

Modified duration = MDURATION(settlement,maturity,coupon,yield, frequency,basis).

Settlement = Date in quotes of settlement.

Maturity = Date in quotes when bond matures.

Coupon = Nominal annual coupon interest rate.

Yield = Annual yield to maturity.

Frequency = Number of coupon payments per year.

1 = Annual.

2 = Semiannual.

4 = Quarterly.

Basis = Day count basis.

0 = 30/360 (U.S. NASD basis). This is the default if the basis is omitted.

1 = Actual/actual (actual number of days in month/year).

2 = Actual/360.

3 = Actual/365.

4 = European 30/360.

Example—Calculating Modified Duration Using Microsoft Excel Calculate the duration and modified duration of a 10-year bond paying a coupon rate of 6 percent, a yield to maturity of 8 percent, and with a settlement date of 1/1/2008 and maturity date of 12/31/2017.

Duration = DURATION("1/1/2008","12/31/2017",0.06,0.08,2) = 7.45

Modified duration = MDURATION("1/1/2008","12/31/2017",0.06,0.08,2)
= 7.16

Note that modified duration is always slightly less than duration, since the modified duration is the duration divided by 1 plus the yield per payment period.

Convexity adds a term to the modified duration, making it more precise, by accounting for the change in duration as the yield changes—hence, convexity is the second derivative of the price-yield curve at the current price-yield point.

Although duration itself can never be negative, convexity can make it negative, since there are some securities, such as some mortgage-backed securities, that exhibit negative convexity, meaning that the bond changes in price in the same direction as the yield changes.

Sensitivity

The sensitivity formula employs *Excel's price formula* along with the duration number for each security. Explanation of the price formula follows:

PRICE(settlement,maturity,rate,yld,redemption,frequency,basis)

- Settlement is the security's settlement date. The security settlement date is the date after the issue date when the security is traded to the buyer.
- Maturity is the security's maturity date. The maturity date is the date when the security expires.
- Rate is the security's annual coupon rate.
- Yld is the security's annual yield.
- Redemption is the security's redemption value per $100 face value.
- Frequency is the number of coupon payments per year. For annual payments, frequency = 1; for semiannual, frequency = 2; for quarterly, frequency = 4.
- Basis is the type of day count basis to use.

Price is calculated as follows:

$$PRICE = \left[\frac{redemption}{\left(1 + \frac{yld}{frequency}\right)^{\left(N-1+\frac{DSC}{E}\right)}} \right] + \left[\sum_{k=1}^{N} \frac{100 \times \frac{rate}{frequency}}{\left(1 + \frac{yld}{frequency}\right)^{\left(k-1+\frac{DSC}{E}\right)}} \right] - \left(100 \times \frac{rate}{frequency} \times \frac{A}{E} \right)$$

where:

DSC = number of days from settlement to next coupon date

E = number of days in coupon period in which the settlement date falls

N = number of coupons payable between settlement date and redemption date

A = number of days from beginning of coupon period to settlement date

■ ■ ■

We hope that you will put the automated e-workbook to good use.

MARILYN COHEN & CHRIS MALBURG

About the Authors

As CEO of Los Angeles–based Envision Capital Management, Inc., **Marilyn Cohen** is one of the top bond managers in the country. Her 30-year financial career has included securities analysis at William O'Neil & Co., bond brokerage at Cantor Fitzgerald, Inc., and for the past 16 years, founder and CEO of Envision Capital Management in Los Angeles. She specializes in managing bond portfolios for individuals. For over 15 years Marilyn has written the bond column appearing in *Forbes* magazine. She is the co-author of *Bonds Now!* (John Wiley & Sons, 2009) and authored *The Bond Bible* (New York Institute of Finance). Additionally, she is a popular guest on CNBC, Fox Business News, PBS, Bloomberg News, and the major broadcast networks. Marilyn's specialty is guiding individuals through the workings of the bond market in plain English.

As founder and managing editor of Writers Resource Group, Inc., **Chris Malburg** is an accomplished financial writer with over four million words in print spread among 11 popular books. Chris is a CPA, has an MBA, and is a former partner at an investment banking firm. Chris' clients and projects span securities broker/dealers, automotive manufacturers, software companies, healthcare companies, and insurance and financial services enterprises.

Together, Marilyn and Chris publish the monthly *Marilyn Cohen's Bond Smart Investor* newsletter for bond investors. You are entitled to a free three-month trial subscription to the newsletter because you have purchased this book. See the last page of this book for instructions on how to get your free three-month trial subscription.

Marilyn and Chris have been happily married for 35 years. Their passion is raising service dogs for the disabled through Canine Companions for Independence (www.cci.org). Marilyn and Chris have raised six CCI puppies. Two have become service dogs with disabled partners; one is now a hospital therapy dog working with Marilyn at the Veteran's Administration Hospital in Los Angeles.

Index

VOLUME 4 / NUMBER 3 / MARCH 2011

MARILYN COHEN'S
Bond Smart Investor

FREE 3-MONTH TRIAL SUBSCRIPTION

Surviving the Bond Bear Market and *MARILYN COHEN'S BOND SMART INVESTOR* Newsletter:...two of today's most powerful tools for bond investors.

Whether you're a novice or a seasoned pro, you cannot afford to be without *Marilyn Cohen's Bond Smart Investor.* Each issue is packed with:

- Muni and corporate bond buy and sell recommendations by CUSIP number
- Porfolio-crushing bond market hazards to watch for
- Proven ways to reduce risk exposure
- Bond funds: Which ones to buy and which to sell

FREE with the purchase of *Surviving the Bond Bear Market* **Forbes** will give you a **FREE** 3-month trial subscription to *Marilyn Cohen's Bond Smart Investor* Newsletter.

Your Satisfaction Guaranteed
If for any reason you are not delighted with your FREE 3-month trial subscription to *Marilyn Cohen's Bond Smart Investor* you are under no obligation to renew at the low annual rate.

To order your **FREE** 3-month trial subscription to *Marilyn Cohen's Bond Smart Investor* newsletter, after purchase of *Surviving the Bond Bear Market* go to the web site, www.newsletters.forbes.com/SurvivingTheBondBearMarket, then follow the directions. **Forbes** will email your FREE trial subscription to you immediately.

ASK QUESTIONS...
DEMAND INFORMATION...
TAKE ACTION.